Principles of Building Local Libraries in Rural Africa

Initiatives contributing to the implementation of the SDGs inquiry in the United Nations; HLPF/ EASG June 2012 Resolutions; "future we want" ... Era of SDGs

Initiative in building local library in Bugwere. Implementation of SDG4

Author; Comfort Onyee

Declaration –

Initiative hands-on in "Principles of Building Local Libraries in Rural Africa", a sensitization for implementation of Sustainable Development Goal; SDG4 – quality education by the United Nations HLPF/ EASG June 2012 resolutions – "future we want"!

This Project was not Created by a Scholar! The skills have developed over time – excellence is what we repeatedly do. When this is the case, you must know this Project took root 1994 from children who questions their parents that why are we living in the Diaspora? Consequently, that developed into a Project idea as stated above, now a volunteer work/ Sensitization, in small groups in rural homeland(s) to advocate for implementation of Mother Language UNESCO-SDG4 quality education, should be in favor of Africa School curriculum Reform to foster the above Subject, based on Africa Spoken Languages reunion with Mother Language in Antiquity. Also recall and quote Nelson Mandela; *("talk to a man in his language and it will go to his Head, talk to a man in the language he understands, and it will go to his Heart")*. Not only, remember Cheikh Anta and Theophile Obenga Symposia UNESCO-Cairo Conference 1974 to confront the UNESCO on the whereabouts of Africa History in the School Curriculum. Recently, the Comparative method by Jean Claude Mboli 2010 prove Africa spoken languages are genetically related languages with Mother Language in Antiquity.

All trademarks, design rights, copyrights, registered names, the logo, the symbols and the references sited remain property of their respective owners. This social research reserves the right to change the focus of this book; shut down; sell; and or change the terms of use at any time as deemed appropriate by the Brian-child; the Project-Team wholly reserves the right to update additional evidence if needed. This additional evidence may be in form of newly revealed historical facts, and or new observations, statistics etc. The research reserves the right to the inputs, delete and or changes required at any time deemed appropriate.

DEDICATION –

To the Youths Who Carry Our Promise for Tomorrow.
grow with knowledge of self; Spoken Languages do not happen at random. Learn the fact that Spoken Languages are born from Mother Language in Antiquity, learn the fact that Spoken Languages have evolved over time. The Language you Speak from Mother Knee has a Mother.

Tackle that trouble that come your way with resilience, and heart, – Trust Enlightenment is the Sun comes back Every Morning Shining Light for Enlightenment in every element with Spirit. Do not let your Soul be soaked in fear of trouble from within u or troubles from without! If you are hurt? That must count. How you take it must count also! Nonetheless, the challenge is; after you are beaten to ground, what next? Cry if tears come to your eyes. But also tell yourself; "I must collect my courage to go, if I lie here and do nothing that is Disgrace to Our Youths who Carry the Promise for Tomorrow – Libation Pour for the Youths. Libation Pour for our daily struggles and understanding. For I and I must rise and go, the problem does not go away if I and I cannot lore together before the morning come. Firstly, Civilization does not begin from where modern humanity stand, neither do Africa Spoken Languages begin from where Modern World Stands? This information remains unknown behind the veil of ignorance. If Humanity lore together, the Youths throw away the veil of ignorance. Consequently, Humanity must review spoken languages all the time from Antiquity to the period of our time and into the future? For this reason, this Project come face to face with the question; what is local library in Africa if Africa Spoken Languages are disoriented from Mother Language in Antiquity?

/ii. ti. m. Htp/

Libation Pour to Ancestors from whom we learn.

Abbreviations

BCOR;	Bugwere Community Outreach
BCE;	Before Common Era
DSD;	Division for Sustainable Development Goals
EASG;	Education Academic Stakeholder Group in United Nations
HLPF;	High Level Political Forum in United Nations
MDG;	Millennium Development Goals
MGoS;	Major Groups and other Stakeholders in SDGs
NGO;	None Government Organization
RBKCL;	Re-Birth of Knowledge Common Law not tradition
SDG;	Sustainable Development Goals
UN;	United Nations
UNESCO;	United Nations Educational, Scientific and Cultural Organization's International World Heritage program.

Transliteration from Ranykemet; Mother Language to English language

/ii. ti. m. Htp/	Welcome in peace.
/Htp di nsw.t/	Opening prayer/ Offering Formula/ Recitation in Ranykemet language at an opening of an event or ceremony. The length and or concept of the /Htp di nsw.t/ depends on the event.
/Km.t/	Black ↔ Coal ↔ Kemet ↔ Fertile Land etc.
/nTr/	Netcheru; God/ Life ↔ infinite ↔ existence, existence cannot exist yet deny the existence does not exist.
/mdw/	Words
/Ra/	using the Gardiner codes, we look in the Vygus dictionary and find N5 is /Ra = Sun or det. hrw, "day" or sw, "day" or N5 Det sun ↔ times ↔ Sun-god ↔ Enlightenment.
/sbA/	To teach, to instruct, to tend
/Saaga/	Saaga
/shm.m. Htp/	Travel in peace.
/sSw/	Scribe ↔ write.
/sSw mdw nTr/	Scribe Divine Words from Netcheru.

Introduction –

You will gather important insight from the Idea "Principles of Building Local Libraries in Rural Africa" firstly; we are living the era of SDGs; Sustainable Development Goals

Pschological Time and Space – when the United Nations HLPF themselves are talking about SDG4 prudently? Stakeholder 996234843-AVwDHA.Org is not into that prejudice. This Project is as Ambitious as a Political Philosopher should with regards, a Stakeholder initiative contributing to the implementation of the SDGs.

– implementation of SDG4 quality education by 2030 must concern School Core-Curriculum Reform in Africa if not everywhere. Colonial languages are a must in Africa from pre-primary to the highest level of education, because of prejudice of United Nations HLPF. Africa Spoken Languages are sister languages with a Mother Language Ranykemet" in Antiquity, just like Indo-European are sister languages, have a mother language "Latin" in Antiquity. No wonder descendants of Indo-European languages tell their History properly, in school they are taught to use and Reason in Indo-European languages with reference to the Mother Language; "Latin" in Antiquity. Same way, SDG4 quality education for Africa Spoken Language have a Mother Language; Ranykemet in Antiquity but HLPF is dead silent about that. Consequently, MGoS contribution to SDGs means little to nothing if, implementation of SDG4 does not emphasize School Curriculum Reform in Africa if not everywhere. If Africa is to Tell Her History Properly, Africa must know and use Africa Spoken Languages with reference to Mother Language; Ranykemet Historical Africa Studies in Sound Law sSw mdw nTr. That is how Indo-European Languages manage to tell their stories well because in school they are taught how language should be learnt and used. That is what HLPF must emphasis to indigenous people concerning implementation of SDG4 quality education by year 2030. Rather than shying away with word like; "an education which includes everybody", "no one left behind" etc. what do you mean by inclusion, but remain dead silent about the importance of spoken languages with reference to the mother language? What do you mean with inclusive society when in global north, where all the United Nations Offices must be based the Pilot questionnaire for inclusive into society is written such that the applicate must be questioned to in such a manner to Feil the interview? So that in future whoever will read that history, will be led to understand that the interviewed was on the wrong, whilst the interviewer keeps the innocent side. Yes, because he or she is so highly educated can see that the interview is (intellectual Acrobatic) written with intent to exclude the interviewed.

Here is the Scenario; by year 2022 he or she who wants to enter to live, work/ research in Africa must enter Africa with at least a Certificate of Knowledge of Ranykemet. Africa School Curriculum Reform Must have start-up phase Year 2022 whereby Ranykemet is taught in every school at all levels in Africa. year 2022 start-up phase for Africa to know a local library is built on Principles of insight in local spoken languages firstly; the Lore, Chants, word creativity etc. told by the natives themselves. So, when written Literature is added to the local library, natives base on knowledge of understanding spoken languages serve us based with reference to mother language. The natives visiting the local libraries will be inspired to do more and advance in language use. Spoken Language in a community serves leaves no one behind. HLPF must know that an education which leaves no one behind is an education that includes human languages ... Read also the Book Title; Mother Language – Our Common Good by Tolofaina KudambangaMwanna 2019.

This Book is update of the Information Seminars Manual prepared by volunteer – 996234843-AVwDHA.Org. Based in Oslo – Norway, daughter organization based in London – United Kingdom and BCOR; Bugwere Community Outreach; a Partner based in Bugwere - Mbale. The Manual is used in sensitization Seminars in Rural Africa. Because of this volunteer work, the Organization in fact learns more from the participants' inputs and questions. That is how the organization discovered what is at stake in Africa education system consequently, what is at stake in Africa leadership! This book is informative and with methods on the way forward to Excellence.

The words; "Saaga" and "Lore" or Oral literature are repeatedly used in this book. Tradition the words are used mostly in historical studies for stories or accounts narrated by word of mouth, with their emphasis on being passed on from one source or generation to another. This Project work will use these words several times to donate the literature, but without any of the prejudice attached to this term.

Chapter 1.

Building Local Library in Rural Africa Must be Initiative Implementation of SDG4 quality Education. Starting from my native Bugwere Folklore Saaga –

Eimerela ..., eimerela ..., eimerela ..., Eimerela ... nolusagaluko omuLutumo oLugwere.
(in English; literary meaning – Peace X4 with Libation Pour in between).

Target group; Youths who Carry Our Promise for Tomorrow. Africa States and Governments; inquiry in the United Nations; HLPF/ EASG June 2012 Resolutions; "future we want" ... implementation of SG4 quality education in Africa

Given the ongoing colonialism school core-curriculum in Africa, Africa Leaders and Africa historians are faced with burden of living Africa behind. Therefore, we must wake-up to the fact that we are living the era of SDGs; Sustainable Development Goals Pschological Time and Space – where many are talking about SDG4 quality education prudently, and quote HLPF[1]; *"Ensure inclusive and equitable quality education and promote lifelong learning opportunities for all"?* Immediate question is what do you mean by inclusion, but remain silent about Africa subconscious in knowledge of spoken language with reference to mother language Ranykemet in Antiquity? If we know better, we do better, same way; Africa must know explicitly, the words in the Africa Spoken Languages on Mother Knee have a Mother Language; Ranykemet in Antiquity. Africa must know why they walk the way they walk. Africa must know why they make the songs they sing, Africa must know why they Embroider and Weave the way they Embroider and Weave is because all this is coming from A Mother Culture in Antiquity – importantly, Africa must know; up-coming leaders in Africa will not succeed if Africa School Curriculum remains the way it is. Upcoming leaders in Africa remain the same product of colonial school, therefore they know no better either. We do better when we know better consequently, implementation of SDG4 quality education introduce School Curriculum Reform, Start-up phase already by Year 2022, not any later.

---

[1] https://sustainabledevelopment.un.org/hlpf/2019

Question;   Where are you going with Bugwere folklore Saaga?

Answer –

Initiative in contributing in implementation of SDGs ... Bugwere Community is my birthplace; the first Spoken Language on my Mother Knee is Lugwere language. Given implementation tool; Mother Language UNESCO-SDG4 quality education, given the United Nations June 2012 resolutions and outcome; "future we want", the right thing to do is – Sankofa, go back and get it. Go back to the Source through Spoken Language on Mother Knee. There is no better way to learn than learning in Spoken Language on Mother Knee.

My attention goes right home – Africa Spoken Languages are disoriented from union with Mother Language; Ranykemet in Antiquity. Indo-European spoken language tell their history properly by bringing in word origin from mother language "Latin" in Antiquity. Indo-European/ Whites are the authors of Project; Missionaries ↔ Colonialism ↔ development aid to Africa, with strategy to disorient Africa spoken languages from union with mother language in Antiquity. Nonetheless, SDGs Pschological Time and Space Must make sense to them that "no one left behind" means Africa Spoken Languages reunion with Mother Language in Antiquity already by Year 2022 Start-up Phase in School Core-Curriculum Reform in Africa if not everywhere. Consequently, implementation of Mother Language UNESCO-SDG4 quality education in Africa opens doors for Africa Spoken Languages reunion with Mother Language in Antiquity.

Importantly, you must Know we are living SDGs Pschological time and space

Consequently, SDG4 quality education in Africa will produce leaders different from the current Africa leaders. Given SDG4 quality education – is pschological time and space to advocate for the Principles of Building Local Libraries in Rural Africa cannot be without Africa Sankofa, go back to the source, the Birth of Knowledge to get the Skills Right for SDG4 quality education.

Descendants of Africa must put on the helm, to be initiative in helping Africa State and Governments with inquiry in the United Nation HLPF/ EASG June 2012 resolutions; "future we want" for Africa; the implementation of Mother Language UNESCO-SDG4 quality education, inevitably means start-up phase for School Curriculum Reform for Africa must begin no later than year 2022. Implementation of SDG4 inevitably means Africa Spoken Languages reunion with Mother Language in Antiquity, inevitably means; he or she who wants to enter to live, work and research in Africa must get a certificate in basic knowledge of Africa Spoken Languages are spoken guided from the Mother Language; Ranykemet, the first written down Language in the history of written literature. Inevitably means; Principles of building local libraries in Africa for Africa to tell Africa History properly. Africa language are spoken from generation to generation guided by association of ideas and as we will see in the workshop Chapter 6.

- In the 21st. century it is no longer a secret Birth of knowledge date back to "Historical Africa" by Cheikh Anta Diop and Theophile Obenga Symposia in UNESCO-Cairo Conference 1974.
- In the 21st. century it is no longer a secret the Birth of Invented Traditions Embedded with Racism and Corruption is White Supremacy then coerce the rest of the world to consume it. with reference to "inversion of traditions" by Hobsbawm and Terrence Ranger PDF 1983.

The scenario is Historical Africa the Birth of Knowledge is where the World "Sankofa"; go back to the Source – Africa Birth of Knowledge, get Skills Right to move forward in Civilization. Contra White Supremacy the Birth of Invented Traditions Embedded with Racism and Corruption is – White Supremacy Survive by Coercing the rest of the World to consume their commodity; the Invented Traditions Embedded with Racism and Corruption. from here you must put records right; corruption is not a thing of the poor. Corruption is strategy of conceptual Western business. You should ask yourself the question; if they donate so much many to agrarian societies for development aid – where does the refund come from? This is how corruption comes to be.

Corruption is not a culture; corruption can be defeated by having equal information on common goods. Corruption will be defeated if our everyday lives and our political lives sit on a round table to challenge and illuminate each other. That is what "Initiative in contributing in implementation of SDGs" should stand for ... Coordinate related Projects to challenge and illuminate in HLPF What is at stack in human society is hiding shareable information from those who need it most. HLPF will gain more than loose if Africa have access to Africa Spoken Language reunion with Mother Language in Antiquity.

The road map to the Principles of building libraries in rural Africa is what this his book is concerned with; Chapter 2; the Context. Chapter 3. The gathering Lore/ literatures and Authors. Chapter 4. Methodology; identified research questions and their assumptions. Chapter 5. The findings and results. Chapter 6. Discussion and Workshop. Chapter 7. Excellence is what we repeatedly do – therefore the Suggested Way Forward.

To enjoy maximum harvest of "Principles to Build Local Libraries in Rural Africa", the reader needs to read Africa Kemet Historians/ linguistic – Cheikh Anta Diop and Theophile Obenga Symposia UNESCO-Cairo Conference 1974 to confront the narrative that the Whites are the originators of Civilization? The reader needs to read the Ten years later "inversion of traditions" by Eric Hobsbawm and Terrance Ranger PDF 1983 – inversion of traditions invaded from elsewhere, institutionalized, ritualized in the Europe and Nordics proof is – invented traditions have a short history and are traceable back to origin in indigenous societies who still practice on their association of ideas. Three decades later came out "Language Comparative Method" Book by Jean Claude Mboli 2010. Originally, this book is written in French. But 2015, Mr. Mboli and two other scholars did a video interview in English YouTube Video; Conversation with Mboli 2010 a research in comparative method. Having watched this video, on can get the insight of how Africa Spoken Languages are genetic sister languages born from a Mother Language in Antiquity.

Jean Claude Mboli 2010 expands Obenga's work 1993 and argues; Africa Spoken Languages are Genetically Sister Languages born from; Negro Kemet Language Family; developed and evolve because of extrusion of the word or vocabulary two different methods for formulating words of which he Mboli describes as; *"Kekwe or kweke"* (as we will see in the Chapters here below) – these are same word, however, the syllables are switched in the case of the first word *"Kekwe"* and then into the other *"kweke"* and then, as a result, of the convergence in history, with migrating groups (see the migrating summary on his language migration diagram hereby attached) … Gathering lore, written literature and association of ideas in Chapter 3. Discussion and Workshop – Chapter 6

2010 Jean-Claude Mboli published a book title; "Origin of Africa Languages. 630 Pages", of Scientific linguistic volume. Recognizing the short-comings and expands Obenga's work. He demonstrates that Obenga was correct! Modern spoken Africa languages are genetically related to Negro Kemet. First, Mboli examined six languages, and then from there he brought in an additional eight languages. And so, he examined all the paradigms; the lexicon, the grammar, and what linguistics call the semantics. Where semantics is your world view – something like; a working tool into the language. All the efforts to build a rigorous procedure for users to apply. So, Mboli is the latest Model based on Obenga 1993.

Who are the Bugwere People?

Native Home base; Bugwere Community in Eastern Uganda, Bugwere Community is a member of Africa Great Lakes Region

Bugwere in culture is a History of Africa Motherhood – Cultural leaders are Elders, Priests, and Guardians and surprisingly the Children.

The history of Bugwere is short and challenging. A majority Bagwere are said to have emigrated to their present area from ⬚⬚⬚ and ⬚⬚⬚, and travelled along ⬚⬚⬚ ⬚⬚⬚, crossing ⬚⬚⬚ ⬚⬚⬚. For this reason, all the people that settled along the shores of Lake Kyoga like; Banyole, Baluli, Bakenye, Belamiogi have a similar language to Lugwere. Bugwere is also made up of Nilotic and Luo percentage. Bugwere initial area of settlement has shrunk considerably as the Jiesu the Bagisu the Badama have pushed the Bagwere's frontiers inwards.

Oh yes, you read it correctly, children are culture leaders

(Author; Rhiannon Stephens)

Bagwere or Bugwere Community is the Bugwere Community Peopling who live on their native land Bugwere in Eastern Uganda. Bagwere people are just as any other ethnic group; Bagwere live together on their native land Bugwere, together Bagwere plant and grow crops and then together they host the farm crops. In Bugwere there is nothing that scares Bagwere like; Not to Care about one another or not to care about Village Matters! Consequentially, in Bugwere Community, Bagwere flock together, Bagwere fight all day long for not to be excluded whatsoever. Consequently, Bagwere Lore together in chant and myth before the morning come as we will see from Chapter 3; the Chants a gathered information in these groups; the first group is lore of Community Matters on Bugwere Courtyard "Home" co-creators' man and woman characteristics and attempt to associate and trace back to Mother Language in Antiquity. The second group is chant is about light of knowledge, inspiration to advocate for the implementation of SDG4 quality education is the Principles of Building Local Libraries in Africa. Advocate for "future we want". The third group is about Love where Bugwere Youths want to enter manhood and womanhood. Youths in Africa are rarely left alone to deal with any matters, what touches Africa youths the youths themselves take initiative to let the community know and as the seminar narrates on, attempt is made to associate to the meaning of love from Africa spoken languages to Mother language in Antiquity. The fourth group is back to the first group; community matters – the majority and the minority may work independently but lore together to reach community decisions. On that notice, the seminar attempts to relate/ associate Bugwere community word for a meeting house in Customary Bugwere to the word for customary meeting houses elsewhere in Africa. In Chapter 6; in the workshop, run the errand etc. the seminar will show-off Africa Association ideas from the Book comparative method; conversation with Jean Claude Mboli 2010.

Bagwere Value their Elders and Praise their Children. Bagwere say that the children are the past, that the children are the present and the future. I recall; growing up in Bugwere on Mother knee, Bugwere assign to children duties during Courtyard ↔ Clan ↔ Community Matters like; in the courses of recitation/ prayers at the commencement of crop plantation. Harvest Festival lead by *(kwakira o'bwitta²)*, importantly if Bugwere regalia Drums – *Namaddu are to be pulled off.* This custom must be Clan ↔ Courtyard related. But other institutions like Schools, Theatres can have access to *Namaddu* which is acting only without Customary obligatory even if these institutions may act on details like Rituals Libation Pour, all the same it simply an act, nothing more.

now, Namaddu is Typically Bugwere Customary Ritual/ Recitation, nonetheless, one fails to understands the *Namaddu* meaning if the learner chooses to study the meaning of Namaddu and Libation Pour. By the way– these twosomes go together. These twosomes are condensed in Bantu Cultural Composition then passed down to Bugwere in relation to Bantu Rituals and entire Africa. A learner studying Namaddu isolated from a cross section of Africa Cultural Embroider and Weave Continuity is because of colonial programming Africa Spoken Languages union with Mother Language in Antiquity ... By the way, before we go too far, we must point to the usual family story time in the evenings by the fireplace or assemble in the *"Kirolero"* House of Clan/ Courtyard matters.

---

² Cerebrating the harvest of millet grain takes lead in Bugwere Harvest Festival

Consequently, one may ask; for whom is this book written, what is the Goal?

Goal; the Context, the Literature, the research questions and their assumptions, the findings and results, the discussion and workshop, the Excellence etc. firstly, Bugwere people should harvest the Lion's share, but no, this is initiative in "future we want" this is advocating for SDG4 quality education This is target the youths and children who carry the promise for tomorrow. Time is right, time is favourable for SDG4 to foster School Core-Curriculum Reform in Africa. Africa is at the start-up phase in writing down Africa languages Consequently, Africa must build local libraries then the immediate question is; on which Principles, and that foster the meaning with Africa Spoken Languages properly studied something that misguided if Africa languages remain disoriented from Mother Language in Antiquity. Therefore, initiative in participatory information seminars in Bugwere lore is simply steppingstones to the Principles of building local libraries and writing down Africa spoken languages union with mother language in Antiquity.

The Target Group is Our Youths Who Carry Our Promise for Tomorrow. Helping Africa States and Governments, to reach the United Nations; HLPF/ EASG June 2012 resolution and outcome – "future we want". And on that notice, your dialogue, your advocacy in this matter is Welcome in peace */ii. t. m. Htp/*to the lore, Chants, Mythology etc. I think that in so doing, there is wisdom there. moreover, here we will see some of the several ways Communities show Ability to Trust the intuitions to Pass down Wisdom in Society, if the future is to Reward Humanity with more, the reward comes from what we invest in. so, why not put on your helm?

By the way, that means we should not overlook, the miseries of life, because we do not what our children to pay for It In future. Keep it in mind that when it is mentioned; initiative in Bugwere lore, it is not news. Pointing to Bugwere folklore simply exemplifies how the first spoken language on the Mother's Knee should be Principle in Africa rural library building. On that notice, and nonetheless, Bugwere people rove to be community minded, that is a peoples' social security whereby nothing is ever separate, including whatever you think is private, including the children – for the children are born for her native community, something Bugwere consider prosperity major. Again, this is not news.

Background –

Bugwere Lore -

Eimerera ..., eimerera ..., eimerera ..., eimerera ... nolusagalukko.

The incentive to create this book developed from way back 1994 from question by Africa children living in the Diaspora Oslo – Norway. Moreover, over 70 percent of people in the Diaspora struggle with this same question. 2011 was just five years away from the close of the MDG2015 era. in the same year, 996234843- AVwDHA.Org; Added Value with Diaspora Home-Away – based in Norway in Partnership with BCOR; Bugwere Community Out-Reach volunteer organization. These two volunteer organizations went into start-up phase with the Project Idea – Building Libraries in Rural Africa, That Project idea developed from the Norwegian State White papers guidelines to civic societies and the in the Diaspora in Norway, why there is need to turn monetary remittance from industrial countries to Broader Project(s) in Agrarian countries.

Challenge(s);   The immediate challenges the volunteer organizations faced were; What is a local library in Bugwere Community without participatory Information Seminars that will sensitize in Bugwere – why and for whom will the local libraries be built, considering, Bugwere is still considered as Oral Literature

Community? how will Bugwere graduate show willingness to study Lugwere Language independent of colonial obligations?

Short answer;   No way, this is going to be possible, firstly; the community has many troubles like farmland shortage, poverty, hunger etc.

Now, with Project Idea of advocating for local libraries in rural Africa in place. And, with the announcement of the SDGs in the year 2015, it was a relief to see SDG4 quality education by 2030 was, it was easy to identify; Mother Language UNESCO-SG4 quality education 2030 as the timely implementation tool if both BCOR and AVwDHA want to make initiative in carrying out information seminars about building local libraries in local communities.

But having knowledge of the above information, does not meet with the solutions to the troubles above mentioned. So, what can we do? Firstly, we are just volunteering in the Project Idea without liquid monies, or other resources. The only tool we have at hand is the gathered information and guideline about why education and development in Africa crumble. So, we came up to the idea that; although Bugwere community is troubled with other things, also Bugwere hunger for information, update and ideas to do old things in new ways. In the form of self-help unconditionally. So, we do advertise openly for this information, talk with local authorities. To maximize security, then locally meet with participants in small groups who may also pass on information to others. Besides, many Africans both on the Continent and Africa in the Diaspora, are an inspiration in the sense of sharing information through On-line Self-Studies etc. through which we discovered Major information that is going to play important role in this seminar, and that is; Peer Video Conversation with Mboli 2010. This You-Tube peer video was discovered through the On-line Studies headed by two Africa Scholars of Africa Mother Language in Antiquity; Harold Johnson (Asar Imhotep) and Wudjau Iry Maat. What we learn from On-line Studies, we share and spread to fellow Africans if Africa is to throw away the veil of ignorance, Africa must learn and update in Historical Africa to tear down the veil of ignorance. The reader too will rejoice to be knowledgeable in Historical Africa if the reader chooses to learn and understand how Africa Spoken Languages have a common Mother Language and the first written down language as Ranykemet Language in Antiquity. Moreover, Ranykemet was first written down 4 245 BCE.

The other motivation comes about with regards; take for example Bugwere youths do contribute in the National Political Platform. This prompts us to go on with these information seminars also to cause awareness in Bugwere politicians that, if Bugwere politicians want to cause change in politics, let them look to hoe the chef changes the Test of Food. The chef changes the ingredients not the stove! Bugwere upcoming politicians and the sitting politicians both prove to be the stoves made in colonial schools who cannot effect change of test of Africa politics, until there is school curriculum reform, Africa politics remains of the same test. So, the right places to look for information for change necessitates that Bugwere politicians advocate for School Curriculum Reform through advocate for implementation of SDG4 and with background of knowledge of Cheikh Anta Diop and Theophile Obenga Symposia UNESCO-Cairo Conference 1974. Diop and Obenga put on a massive symposium in the UNESCO-Cairo Conference to confront the White Supremacy Egyptology Narrative that White Supremacy is the Origin of Civilization. This narrative is used by White Supremacy to keep Africa under their control in the name of development aid firstly to Africa and then elsewhere to hide their agenda. That is how the history of enslavement, missionaries, colonialism and currently the ongoing White Supremacy NGOs in Africa. To disorient Africa Spoken Language union with Mother Language in Antiquity (see Diop himself in picture here attached);

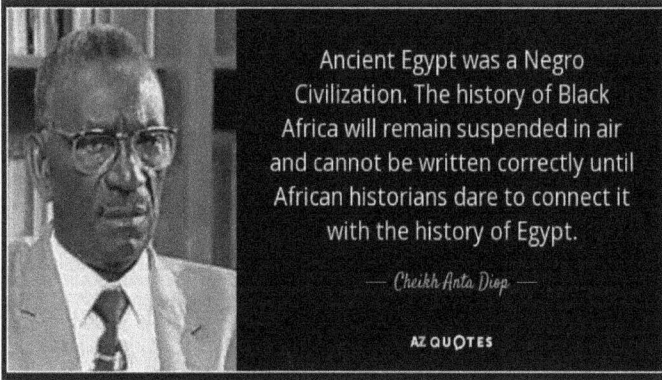

Ancient Egypt was a Negro Civilization. The history of Black Africa will remain suspended in air and cannot be written correctly until African historians dare to connect it with the history of Egypt.

— *Cheikh Anta Diop* —

AZ QUOTES

Diop 1973

"When we say that the ancestors of the Blacks, who today live mainly in Black Africa, were the first to invent mathematics, astronomy, the calendar, sciences in general, arts, religion, agriculture, social organization, medicine, writing, technique, architecture; that they were the first to erect buildings out of 6 million tons of stone (the Great Pyramid) as architects and engineers—not simply as unskilled laborers; that they built the immense temple of Karnak, that forest of columns with its famed hypostyle hall large enough to hold Notre-Dame and its towers; that they sculpted the first colossal statues (Colossi of Memnon, etc.)—when we say all that we are merely expressing the plain unvarnished truth that no one today can refute by arguments worthy of the name". **Cheick Anta Diop 1973**

Ten years later, Eric Hobsbawm and Terrence Ranger PDF 1983 comes in to advocate for Africa wake-up from dogma slumber! Africa Leadership is crumbled to the ground because Africa has been hit hard by White Supremacy Inversion of Traditions and quote –

"Interestingly from our point of view – inversion of traditions is the use of ancient materials to construct invented traditions of a novel type for quite a novel purpose. A large store of such materials is accumulated in the past in any ancient society and an elaborated language of symbolic practice and communication is always available. Sometimes new traditions could be readily grafted on old ones. Sometimes they could be devised by borrowing from the well supplied warehouses of official ritual symbolism and moral exhortation – religious and princely pomp, folklore and freemasonry (itself an earlier invented tradition of Great Symbolic Force[3])
... **Eric Hobsbawm and Terrance Ranger PDF 1983**

It is said that of the 100 % Human Race, the White Supremacy adds up to 22% of which Europe makes 16% and Arab is the other 6% of White supremacy. Reference *(January 2018 Racism debate Oslo Norway, by Johan Galtung Q and A)* interestingly by January 2019, a year later Johan Galtung removed his video with 996234843-AVwDHA.Org from YouTube – let it be known that in that debate 996234843-AVwDHA.Org came-up with 7 minutes input Q& A to Johan Galtung; Norwegian Senior Research in NGO PRIO-Norway.

See also AVwDHA in 28th Nov 2017 Uppsala University Lecture on Africa Poverty – where our input is to Africa upcoming leaders, unless find ways to learn about and have knowledge of Africa Worldview, you will never tell Africa history properly. And if you tell Invented Traditions to Africa is the history of Africa, then you have fallen into the trap of white supremacy consequently you remain behind the veil of ignorance in Africa Worldview. https://www.youtube.com/watch?v=Q5Gk36pUu1k

Back to the point, of course there are many pieces of knowledge out there, but if Africa remains behind the veil of ignorant in Africa History, if Africa does not study and write Africa Spoken languages as sister languages with a common mother in Antiquity. Africa troubles will simply continue as a mess on Africa face. Africa should stop listening to the

---

[3] http://staff.washington.edu/ellingsn/Hobsbawm_Inventing_Traditiions.pdf

United Nations without emphasizing the question of the United Nations June 2012 resolutions and outcome – "future we want" consequently, implementation of Mother Language UNESCO-SDG4 quality education is Africa demand for School Core-Curriculum, so that Africa Children and Youths get an education that focus on Africa heritage and development. That is how Change in leadership in Africa will happen. Nelson Mandela said –

> *"If you talk to a man in a language he understands, that goes to his head. If you talk to him in his language, that goes to his heart.*' Nelson Mandela;

Diop, Obenga Symposia UNESCO-Cairo Conference 1974; the History, Education and Development of Africa will remain suspended in Air and cannot be written correctly until Africa themselves dare to connect with Africa History in Antiquity. Moreover, there are many more scholars who argue Africa must get off education development aid forms written for Africa by foreigners to Africa –

UNDERSTANDING THE BAD NEWS OF "INVERSION OF TRADITIONS" ON THE AFRICA GRADUATE –

"African politicians, cultural nationalists and, indeed, historians are left with two ambiguous legacies from the colonial invention of traditions. One is the body of invented traditions imported from Europe which in some parts of Africa still exercises an influence on ruling class culture which it has largely lost in Europe itself! As for historians, they have at least a double task. Africa must free themselves from the illusion that the African custom recorded by officials or by many anthropologists is any sort of guide to the

African past. But they also need to appreciate how much invented traditions of all kinds have to do with the history of Africa in the twentieth century and strive to produce better founded accounts of them than this preliminary sketch"; **PDF; Eric Hobsbawm and Terence Ranger 1983**

Peer video; Conversation with Mboli 2010 methodically as earlier mentioned, this methodology ague; Africa spoken languages are genetically sister languages from a Mother Language in Antiquity. A calling to pay attention to Diop, Obenga Symposia UNESCO-Cairo Conference 1974. If viewer gets the point in conversation with Mboli 2010, then the reader is guided to see how and why Africa spoken languages are genetically related languages from a Mother Language in Antiquity. Obviously, the reader will get the point of lore Saaga is steppingstone to Africa Spoken Language reunion with Mother Language in Antiquity as Chapter 3 will reveal. And that should bring us to the knowledge of the idea that building local libraries in rural Africa necessitates to sensitize in rural Africa through engaging grassroots to actively recite at Africa Chants, lore, mythology etc. while the library literature goes on in the 21st. century. By the way, 21st. century is time Africa should no longer be tolerant to development aid whose aim is to disorient Africa from Historical Africa. Consequently, if Bugwere need to understand Lugwere Language did not just happen overnight, with evidence; the word "Bagweere[4]" meaning in the language itself has more than one meaning or function. Consequently, if Bagwere youths are to bring change in Politics, there is need to start from School curriculum reform. These are huge Advocates of Change in Africa Leadership, why won't we pay them some Attention?

Why Africa need School Core-Curriculum Reform

---

[4] Bagweere in Lugwere Language meaning is "invaded"

Recall –

The Chef knows; test of food does not change by changing the cooking stove. Change of test of food will be if the Chef changes the ingredients. Consequently, if Africa Youths Want to Change Africa Politics, first we need to advocate for change of School Core-Curriculum by implementation of SDG4 quality education by 2030

The Comparative Method in African Linguistics by Jean Claude Mboli –

Comparative Method by Jean Claude Mboli 2010 etc are methodology books Teaching; Spoken Languages prove to be genetically sister languages, which have evolved from a Stem Mother Language in Antiquity –

Africa linguistics advise us that the challenge in Africa is the issues with Africa languages. Africa Languages have not been written in the interest of Africa for the last 3100 years. The History of Africa has suffered exclusion from textbooks the last 3 100 years. So, in this 21st. century, we of Africa descendant, what do we do now? Yes, we must DEAL with it, first, Africa History is very long and complex. Africa history is as Old as the first Mankind on the Mother Earth. We of Africa, among others, we must re-think from the first spoken language on Mother knee, compare with Mother language in Antiquity as well as Africa sister languages. This is how linguistics for example Jean Clause Mboli, Mubabinge Bilolo, Cheikh Anta Diop, Theophile Obenga...

Where do we start if we want to build a local library in Bugwere?

If this is the case, different people will come with different ideas, but here is the one we share – the primary place to begin is the first spoken language on mother's knee. In this case the local library building in Bugwere should stand on the pillars of Lugwere Language ... in this 21st. century Africa must continue to wake-up to self-determination to recover lost memory of how Africa Spoken Languages were born and evolve. Participatory in information seminars in local communities and in the interest of how to advocate to build local library must develop from Spoken language of that community, this idea creates room for people in the community to participate. This is of two advantages, firstly this comes with job creation. Secondly, from a peoples' participation – research questions and their assumptions are born. Related ideas as well as new Ideas are born from the local people themselves. Take for example; we often hear Africa people talk about building roads that connect Africa Countries. If the reader here is paying attention, already we can see how participatory information seminars in this regard, bring the several ideas close to the participatory Minds. In the course of the Project, participant can begin to realise how road building in Africa relates with building local libraries in rural Africa. This is how to create quality jobs etc. So, let us inspire Africa children, parents, grandparents and great grandparents come out to with lore while writing down the books that will stand on those bookshelves must be firstly written from within. Africa will wake up and be proud of participating in writing books founded from Africa Worldview.

Neither missionaries nor colonialism nor White Supremacy NGOs find it wise to support Africa wakeup to Knowledge of understanding that; "what the word public library stands for" is word of mouth/ speech or Folklore turned into script by a native people. So, if you, the other one over there and I in this regard, put our efforts together. Education and Library building will serve a native Africa lore. The same incentives should be everywhere in Uganda and the entire Africa Continent build schools Libraries based on Africa Worldview, instead of imitating education forms from outside Africa. The same incentives should be embarrassed by also both donor nations and development aid patterner Nations that 43 years following the 1974 Diop and Obenga in UNESCO Cairo Conference, is hardly known of by Africa people themselves, and that is ridiculous, because here is the World laughing at Africa for being the only ethnic people who read and write invented tradition education systems brought to Africa from the near recent despite the presence of Historical Africa Worldview! following the 1974 Diop and Obenga in UNESCO Cairo Conference.

By the way, the United Nations June 2012 resolutions and outcome; "future we want". Must deliver what they advertise. Africa, we need solutions and answers to bring to SDG 2030... If you come to think about it, it makes sense that; we do not have to wait until 2030 before it is on every African's lips that Africa languages are sister languages genetically related and with a single stem mother language with currently given name is Negro Egyptian! Rural Africa should be a part of the SDGs discuss aiming from participation-seminars on saga Africa mother language. Consequently, Africa Spoken Languages need to do a reunion with Mother Language in Antiquity. Africa, we need to organize and re-organize to go back to the source; Mother Language in Antiquity to get the Skills right. Africa herself cries out for change in Politics and Leadership. But that cannot be unless Africa come to see that change in Africa will happen by Introduction of Education Core-Curriculum based on Africa Worldview. Consequently, Africa needs to organize and reorganize; put hands on to sensitize local communities in Africa Spoken Languages Reunion with Mother Language in Antiquity. This is the way and the idea how Africa Education, Politics and Leadership will realise "future we want". Take for example; "one cannot change the Test of Food by Changing the Stove! It is by change of ingredients that change the test of food. Same thing; Africa Education, Politics and Leadership Must Waken up to Knowledge of understanding how Africa Spoken Languages reunion with Mother Language in Antiquity Contributes to better Education ↔ better Politics ↔ better Leadership. Then, the World or Africa for that matter will be looking forward to "future we want" ... Please share with us your dialogue and your advocacy.

Objective –

Africa, we need to strive for Africa Spoken Languages reunion with Mother Language in the era of SDG - indeed Mother Language UNESCO-SDG4 quality education by 2030! In Africa's case; Africa we need school curriculum reform looking to Africa Worldview. BCOR volunteer work for Go Back to School Sensitization, in small groups in rural homeland(s) concerning Mother Language SDG4 for Quality Education. Consequently,

BCOR sees SDG4 connection with – Nelson Mandela quote *("talk to a man in his language and it will go to his Head, talk to a man in the language he understands, and it will go to his Heart")*, connection with regards – Diop, Obenga Symposia UNESCO-Cairo Conference 1974 and Conversation with Mboli 2010 that Africa spoken languages are genetically related languages from a Mother Language in Antiquity

Say; Yes, to Folk-Lore Saaga participatory seminars, a starting point to help the student identify research question from mother languages that is how the student will be guided to look for the sources of the research questions which Necessitates to travel back in time, happily the end result is the Answers to the research question are to be found nowhere else other than in genetic sister languages and Mother Language in Antiquity. Participatory seminars at grassroots is one way to go about it, so that Africa people themselves are engaged in the literature gathering. So that when the scholars do the comparative method for example the comparative method by Jean Claude Mboli 2010 diagram; the stages dating back to Neo sound law to Proto Classical Negro Kemet – modern Africa will clearly see and understand what and why this and that cultural ceremony is performed the way it is. Africa will understand why they are very good at Religions, through Reason rather than believe.

Back to the point; if we really mean seriously about SDG4 by 2030. If the Idea of building local libraries in rural Africa and the idea of building roads to connect Africa countries are from Africa initiative, this will cause Africa to think quality jobs and in turn that will prompt Africa advance to middle income standard. Because, many will walk away from marginalized jobs to quality jobs. Too many jobs are locked up if Africa spoken languages remain limited to Oral Literature. Volunteer in sensitization in rural Africa to argue; Africa Spoken Languages reunion with Mother Language and back to the School Core-Curriculum Books! We must go help Africa State and Governments Rethink; "future we want" depends on the School Curriculum Reform.

If we prove to be rigorous at these information seminars, we stand the chance to build and Protect local library Building in Native Homes. So, welcome home, Africa Spoken Languages reunion with Mother Language in Antiquity by Africa themselves must serve us both culturally and institutionally. Africa is wealthy of human factor resources and Africa lore material factor. Next is why not start-up? Rural Africa deserve to know what libraries are built for and to know that libraries, museums galleries etc. firstly these are built to present native to the future generation. Then perhaps, outsiders also.

Strategy –

Recommended Strategy

Knowledge of Africa Mother Language Will set us free from pseudo scholarship, and re-orient us to Educations' purpose how can we do this? – Well, let us spread information about the existence of the Language Comparative Method by Jean Claude Mboli

Goals

- Striving for quality jobs – via Africa Spoken Languages reunion with Mother Language in Antiquity
    - o Build up through presenting participatory seminars and workshop for Folklore Saaga
    - o Engage ourselves practically researching in the language learnt on the Mother's Knee through reciting at folklore. With that we make available something to engage with, job creation for adults as well as inspire youths and children to do Africa Classic Studies. BCOR do believe; local libraries in rural Africa will create jobs but first a people must come out to recite at folklore to donate to the meaning with local library.
    - o Round off with a recommendable test to motivate participants NOT to be time wasting.

Guidelines;

Five (5) steps adopted from Africa centricity by BCOR and involve in collect folklore saga
–

- Considers that no phenomena must be apprehended adequately, without locating it first. A phenol must be first studied and analysed in relationship to psychological time and space. So, when we are analysing something, we must keep chronology in our mind and geography. Where they are at (located). So, when we are talking of local language e.g. Lugwere is a spoken language in Eastern Uganda. At what time and certainties of world view? Certainly, after the migrating from Toro and Bunyoro Kingdoms in Western Uganda. So, we must locate it first.

- Participatory Seminars in Saga Folklore should consider the folklore a phenomenon to be divorce, dynamic, and in motion and therefore, it is necessary for a person to accurately know the phenomena even midst of fluctuations. Participatory Seminars in Folklore saga is a form of cultural critique that examines "*etymological*"use of words and terms so that all participants learn (know) the source and for further analysis. Because the words we use to describe things help us to know the word source. For example, in this book Prompt examination of some Lugwere words mentioned in the book' literature, the chosen words are (Saaga, Bagwere/ Bagweere, Kirolero and Libation Pour) the details will be indicated in chapter 4; identified research questions and assumptions, Chapter 5; Findings and Results, Chapter 6; Discussion and Workshop Chapter 7; Excellence and the way forward etc.

- Participatory Seminars for Folklore Saga will aid Africa to uncover the masks behind the foreign rhetoric of power, position, and privilege to Africa, and how the rhetoric establishes the politics that miss-treat Africa History, Culture and Development.

- Participatory Seminars in Folklore Saga automatically creates imaginative structure of the system of economics, bureau-politics, policies of government expressional cultural form in the attitude, direction, and language of the phenol! Be it text, institutional, or institutional personality, direction or invent.

When this is the case, folklore Saaga is sold pillars in inspiration to go back to school, quality jobs creation and building of libraries in your rural community based on knowledge of self. Coming from not a follow the money Project, we will find difficulty to get peoples' attention, but we are confident people change, consequently, the right thing to do is the seminar to be equipped with sure knowledge in the information seminar presentation. One participant will tell friend who will tell friend etc. We have some Africa custom wisdom to be tolerant. The seminar is not intended to coerce a people to change. Rather the seminar intends to inspire a people to pick-up oneself go back to school or look for available means to learn old things anew. Shed light for your social milieu on the principles of building local libraries in rural Africa to mark the distinctions to know what is going on in our cultures verses what is going on in other cultures. Because Participatory Seminars in Folklore Saaga aim is to build local library that serves a people firstly in the Africa spoken language and to awaken a people come back to Africa-consciousness.

How did we come to this idea anyway?

- The chants/ folksongs from childhood, keep coming back in memory, growing up in home community Bugwere, through chants communication, loads of work can be accomplished, loads of books can be read etc. now with the announcement of SDG4 quality education … it is possible for rural Africa comeback forgotten workplaces. Consequently, we need to organize and reorganize to shape the future for our children in our communities.

Word of inspiration

It is not by the size that we succeed. It is by striving that we succeed. However short a man may be, he has potential to see the sky. Do not let yourself become psychologically programmed off the knowledge of self!

Love thy-self, trust thy-self balance your Mind -Sun Light comes back every glorious morning, a means to enlightenment of self. implementation of SDG4 is for us to rise our concern for Africa gender co-creativity as we will see here below.

Options available are such as –

- Study, study, study, and study. Never say never, update is timeless phenomenon. Remember to keep the local authority informed, and to first get permission before doing public seminars.
- Secondly, we should seek monetary funds in alternative places, e.g. doing charity works for other people or firms. If we get token pay save it to fund the bigger dream.

The advantages and the disadvantages of each option as above –

Loss of personal life, loss of old friends, and risk of your belongings; like liquid money, time investment etc. you gain higher Spirit over the oppressors. To be an oppressor is to become low at Spirit. This is how the Africa race survive the oppressor.

Determine the cost of each option –

This is going to cost you your personal life, loss of old friends and much more. All you be left with is the difficulty to learn how to do the same things anew! Almost no one is going to believe in you. However, people change, so, learn to be tolerant. Importantly learn that it is useless to hold on to disagreements and disappointments as well as old loss. Practice on feeling things and then let go!

Recommendations

Recommend one or more of the strategies

- Classical language of Africa people and why we need to study the source.
- Knowledge of Africa Spoken Languages reunion with Mother Language in Antiquity will set us free from pseudo scholarship, and re-orient us to Educations' purpose.
- Enrol at a Seshew Medew Netcher - True Aspiring Scribes of Divine Words, and Foster and participate at general information seminars in your first spoken language on mother knee, so that general knowledge and practice on how we apply everyday language becomes inspiration for youths and children, and other people engaged in Africa studies.

If things turn up as expected and understanding

If we succeed from here, then we have gained new ways of looking at life, how to create more jobs, and what it means to develop in local society with your contribution. What a local library means if we are part of the written literature in our mother tongue, then we contribute to the building of the local libraries in native community.

Chapter 2.

Context –

The Context of the "Principles of Building Local Libraries in Rural Africa" has developed from 1994 the crucial questions Africa children in the Diaspora ask their parents; "why are we living in the Diaspora"? Parents are left to scrunch heads in search of answers and solutions to the question. In the Diaspora, it is rare to live with a settled Mind. A long the way, miraculously, the question turned out like this; "Africa the Origin of Civilization"; Cheikh Anta Diop 1973 who will teach my son about the struggles from Historical Africa – known as Pharaonic Kemet (km.t)

"The Spiritual and Scientific founding elements of modern civilization, namely law, knowledge of the matter (mathematics, general and quantum physics, chemistry, medicine, surgery etc.) environment (history, geography, geophysics etc.) and the cosmos (astronomy, cosmology etc.) are rooted in Kemet Civilization"; **Diop 1973**

Historical Africa Context

The near recent history of Africa adopting foreign languages as official languages, is on a conservative average, at least 3 100 years. Interpreted, this means that Africa has experienced three thousand years of cumulative detachment and the obviously adverse effects of disconnect from the resourcefulness and tools of indigenous Africa that automatically come with healthy connection to indigenous languages. As mentioned earlier, this was and still is an intentional strategy of the concept and principle of inversion of traditions and as well expounded in the Research; "invented of traditions; PDF; Eric Hobsbawm and Terence Ranger 1983".

In contrast to invented tradition of education to Africa, the history of education of Africa Worldview before the Inversion is replete with evidence of the ability, capacity and resourcefulness of African indigenous educational systems and languages to solve Africa problems. For example, African (indigenous) educational systems then, produced graduates who built Modern Civilization; Educational Institutions, Federations, Great Kingdoms and various forms of organizations effectively resolved the challenges and problems of their time with no intervention of foreign development aid. So, what is the effect of this foreign aid in other words inversion of traditions?

The effect of the development aid commonly so-called means that genuine and speedy African development is and will always be compromised to distortion and unproductive because the effect of Inversion of Africa turned into Colonialism/ "invented traditions" to Africa and continue to be the case.

But then, in the 21st. century given the tools of implementation; Mother Language UNESCO SDG4 – quality education by 2030 and the tool of implementation of the United Nations June 2012 resolutions and outcomes "future we want" here in specific resolution 183 concerning Africa ... these Tools must take effect here and now. Firstly, to put re-writing of history in check consequently abolish inversion of traditions. The inversion of tradition is a negative complex mechanism embedded with corruption and racism – undoubtedly, the inversion of traditions embedded with racism and corruption is Western Scholars mechanism to coerce the world recognize the Western to be the center of civilization as historical facts continue to unfold in 21st. century. Not only historical facts, even the integration pilot questionnaire in the Western prove to be a questionnaire of guilty conscious incentive. How? The Western integration pilot questionnaire id dedicated to knowing everything about the rest of the World, while hiding who the Western is in terms of the history of their invented traditions. Unfortunately, this forces them to be suspicious people, but the only one they need to be afraid of is the only idea they invented; "inversion of tradition embedded with racism and corruption. Unfortunately, this is the case because of the Western being in denial of common-sense truth Africa is the cradle of civilization.

Political, Cultural and Spiritual Context

Missionaries

Foreign missionaries institutionalized the use of their languages in the educational institutions that they built. The output of this educational process was the replacement of the indigenous mind with the foreign. Along with this replacement was the loss of-

and or detachment with the resourcefulness, tools and ingenuity that are inherent in indigenous culture of which indigenous language is an integral part. For example, the typical graduate of an African educational system considers everything indigenous as inferior to all things foreign.

So, what is the effect of this graduate to African development today? this graduate will always consider foreign solutions as the appropriate solutions to Africa problems while being permanently blind to the resourcefulness of indigenous Africa. This is a subject that is covered in depth in the book "African Nationalism" by Ndabaningi Sithole 1959

Additionally, what is the effect of this educational system on the graduate and consequently to indigenous Africa culture? Another equally adverse effect of this educational system on the graduate is the creation of a distorted African identity in all its aspects be it at a personal, social or any other level. This has one its most clear demonstrations in the graduate refusing to embrace his or her African identity. In other words, this educational system produces, consciously or unconsciously, an enslaved mind because the effect the of this education system is to gradually and ultimately detach its graduates from their indigenous identity, culture, language and all the other resources and tools that are inherent in the indigenous culture.

The Spiritual Context

Another, just as cruel, adverse effect of this educational system is a graduate who by virtue of detachment from the indigenous culture is consequently divorced from the spiritual resources inherent in the culture. In other words, this graduate is Spiritually powerless because the inclination, consciously or otherwise, but mostly unconsciously, is to embrace the adopted tradition or religion which is simply imitation of indigenous religions; and that is to say; "inversion of traditions" – something Eric Hobsbawm and Terrance Rangers explain very well in "inversion of traditions PDF 1983".

Historically, indigenous Africa education systems strengthened the connection of the students to the Spiritual resource inherent in the culture. This ensured that the graduates were well prepared to be resilient in weathering the inevitable tests of life that come in the form of life's hardships. This is not the case of the typical graduate of the current African education system. Because the inclination is to look for help from outside Africa. sadly, this is the case whether that graduate is in or outside Africa.

Africa's education system must produce resilient graduates. Therefore, it is the strongly held argument of this social research that, to produce a graduate that is resilient, Africa's education system requires Africa Worldview to produce a graduate who is resilient.

it is imperative that the implementation of these tools below,

- Mother Language UNESCO SDG4 quality education by 2030 and
- the United Nations June 2012 resolutions; "future we want[5]"

Colonialism Context –

With colonialism came the adoption of foreign languages as official languages of respective Africa countries at the expense of advancement of indigenous language as official languages. This was an intentional strategy to dis-empower Africa from the inbuilt resourcefulness that comes with a healthy attachment from Mother language to daughter languages. This is a subject that is covered in depth in the book "African Nationalism" by Ndabaningi Sithole 1959

Development aid context

How development aid of education in Africa works to the exclusion of Africa culture in Africa. Active participation in courses/ seminars and conferences in global north, soon one comes to realize that, the Africa adjustment to read Africa from foreign languages coerce Africa to self-destruction, because their education development aid to Africa the questions are not concerned with the absence of Africa spoken languages union with Mother Language in Antiquity and missing from school core-curriculum. Now this is

[5] https://sustainabledevelopment.un.org/index.php?menu=1298

development problem. That is hurting on our part Africa descendants if education development aid condition Africa to detach herself from her authentic and ancestral identity, give-up on who Africa is – while adapting to the Authors of inversion of traditions who they are. The technical advancement of Africa education and development should be based on Africa Worldview; Africa Birth of Knowledge Source –

Historical Africa is where mother language our common good and the birth of knowledge happened, and the place to go back to for a rebirth of knowledge. In the 21st century, during the United Nations resolution; "future we want" – it will be development jeopardy from HLPF/ EASG's part if Africa spoken languages remain dis-attached from mother language in Antiquity and are not as part of the School core-curriculum reform by the year 2022.

The Birth of knowledge

Africa Cradle of Civilization. Africa in Antiquity is where early man gave birth to knowledge – aided by the Eye-Mind coordination. The Eye-Mind coordination was early man's road map in exploration and migration. Early man kept on moving and establish daughter cultures in this Great Nation Mother-Earth. Early-man made Historical journey to migrate nTr - the home of plenty, go out there in the emptiness, explored, but Early-man made up his mind and never went back to nTr this is how the history goes according to the evolutionary side of the history on the one hand. On the other hand, is the Bible history on the word of God – the Bible says; and then the Lord God sent Adam on Earth. But when Adam felt lonely, he made a U-turn to the Lord God to ask for someone to keep him company. Then Lord God gave Eve to help Adam with glory to go live in Paradise multiply and fill Mother Earth and have dominion over everything on Earth. These are the two histories about birth of knowledge.

Now, whichever side of the history one may choose, Birth of Knowledge took place long time ago in Africa. Whether one wants to relay on the evolution history, or the Word of

God written in the Bible. Both Histories took place in Africa. what divides these two histories is the time period and below are some references;

> *"the long chronology (based on the available data provided by the Kemetic priest Herodotus and Manetho; place the beginning at ca. 17 000 years BCA). And the short chronology of modern are obligated to admit that by 4245 BCA. Kemet had already invented the Calendar (which necessarily needed or requires thousands of years to develop)"*; **Diop 1973**.

Now, meanwhile Kemetic priest Herodotus and Manetho; place the beginning at ca. 17 000 years BCE - Historical Bible begins with Abraham the father of the Bible History, Abraham was born in present day Iran moved to Africa to drink from the fountain of birth of knowledge and then started documenting the Bible 2000 BCA. Consequently, it is from such information we come to learn how birth of knowledge happened and from which Re-birth of knowledge became common law.

You must get history right; "inversion of traditions" is not custom/ common law. On the other hand, a rebirth of knowledge is custom/ common law.

Rebirth of Knowledge

- Rebirth of knowledge is custom.
- Renaissance is custom.
- What a True Judge in the courtroom does is Custom.

Rebirth of knowledge – is Sankofa, go back to the source of birth of knowledge to get the Skills –

> ➤ *Abraham father of the Bible 2 000 BC went back to Africa Nile Valley to get the Skills Right.*
> ➤ *the Persians 525 BC went back to Africa Nile Valley to get the skills right*
> ➤ *Alexander 333 BC, the Greco Romans with Julius Caesar 50 BC,*

> *the Arabs; seventh century*
> *the Turks in the sixteenth century*
> *the French with Napoleon and then the English at the end of the nineteenth century ...*
> *Nevertheless, it would long continue to initiate the younger Mediterranean peoples; Greco-Roman among others into the Enlightenment of Civilization from the source; Africa in Antiquity.*
> *Throughout in Antiquity as well as modern world, Africa remains the classic land where the contemporary world goes on Pilgrimage to drink at the Fountain of scientific, religious, moral and social knowledge, the most ancient knowledge of mankind will forever acknowledge,* Africa origin of Civilization – **Myth or Reality; Cheikh Anta Diop 1973**.

Custom/ common law must not be confused or interchanged with "tradition"
–

- The wig and gown the judge wear in court **is tradition** not custom.
- Napoleon sitting on Pharaonic Throne **is tradition** not custom.

"Tradition" in this instance is the institutionalized; the ritualized surrounding their substantial action; Eric Hobsbawm and Terence Rangers; PDF – inversion of traditions 1983.

("Eric Hobsbawm and Terence Ranger 1983; refers to modern societies and that includes, the region Europe and Nordic as Traditional Societies. The object and characteristic of traditions in those societies, including invented ones, is seen how inconsistence or invariance show off. The past, real or invented, to which they refer imposes fixed (normally formalized) practices, such as repetition. In modern societies, rituals are Traditions! In short; rituals in modern societies are responses to novel situations which take the form of reference to old situations, or which establish their own. But in most cases these Traditions are the rituals commonly invented, constructed and formally instituted, emerging in a less easily traceable manner within a brief, and dateable period a matter of a few years perhaps- and establishing themselves with great rapidity").

21st. century time is here for Africa graduate to do Custom; Sankofa[6] go back to Pharaonic km.t to drink from the Fountain of Knowledge, get the skills right to move

---

[6] Sankofa is a word in Akan language in Ghana it is also a name of a bird and literary means go back and get.

forward. The works by hand of early man who Migrated from nTr; the place of plenty to establish society, did it with sense for "future we want". Consequently, need to go back to the source to get the skills right, is "future we want".

Chapter 3.

Gathering Bugwere Lore, Written Literature and Authors –

The seminar will go ahead starting with Bugwere Lore/ Chants. Which is also Bugwere Custom; in Bugwere the host bind to the guest through lore/ chant telling. So, relax, sit back listen and then we move forth and back between the lore and written text by linguistic from elsewhere none stop until we bring in reference from Mother Language Ranykemet in Antiquity.

Tube be iimerela no lusagalukko e Bagwere –

E'iimerela ..., eiimerela ..., eiimerela ..., eimerela ..., nolusagalukko.

Bugwere Chant elaborating "a marriage" is union for co-creating –

A maisso ga mugeni gatisya

The Bachelor;	A maisso go mugeni gatisya
Participants;	Aaa aaa banage, a maisso go mugeni gatisya nga o'bula mukali yasumba.
The Bachelor;	Maisso go mugani gatisya
Participants;	Gatisya ngo o bula mukali e yasumba.
The Bachelor;	Akko munsakka kabulya.
Participants;	Maisso go mugeni.
The Bachelor;	Katti ozwainaaaaa ...
Participant;	Maisso go mugeni gatisya ngo'bulla mukali eyasumba.
The Bachelor;	Ako kulwinggi kagudya.
Participants;	Maisso go mugeni.
The Bachelor;	Katti weserekkeeeee ...
Participants;	Maisso go mugeni gatisya ngobula mukali eyasumba.
The Bachelor;	Ne bwoba no nkonko toolye.
Participant;	Maisso go mugeni
The Bachelor;	Toolyeee ...
Participants;	maisso go mugeni gatisya ngo' obula mukali eyasumba.

The Bachelor;	Ne bwoba no mbuli toolye.
Participants;	Maisso go mugeni
The Bachelor;	Toolyeee …
Participants;	Maisso go mugeni gatisya ngo' obula mukali eyasumba.
The Bachelor;	O maama a kangire ndalya.
Participants;	Maisso go mugeni
The Bachelor;	Ndalyaaa …
Participants;	Maisso go mugeni gatisya ngo' obula mukali eyasumba.
The Bachelor;	O baba a kangire ndanywa.
Participants;	Maisso go mugeni
The Bachelor;	Ndanywaaa …
Participants;	Maisso go mugeni gatisya ngo' obula mukali eyasumba.
The Bachelor;	Banange musirike mbalonserye.
Participants;	Maisso go mugeni
The Bachelor;	Nze mbula'o mukali mbonna bingi
Participants;	Maisso go mugeni gatisya ngo' obula mukali eyasumba.
The Bachelor;	Kukyanga kuti njaba kulima.
Participants;	Maisso go mugeni
The Bachelor;	Olwenzwa'e yoo, njanikka tulo "bulo"
Participants;	Maisso go mugeni gatisya ngo' obula mukali eyasumba.
The Bachelor;	Olwemala'e kyo njabba maizzi.
Participants;	Maisso go mugeni
The Bachelor;	Obwenkwatta ensuwa nta kwisule.
Participants;	Maisso go mugeni gatisya ngo' obula mukali eyasumba.
The Bachelor;	Olwenzwa'e yooooo golwo kusya.
Participants;	Maisso go mugeni
The Bachelor;	O'bwitta no male'o mira byere.

Participant;	Maisso go mugeni gatisya ngo' obula mukali eyasumba.
The Bachelor;	Banange ei dembe eidembe
Participants;	Kyakka eidembe!
The Bachelor;	Banange ei dembe eidembe
Participants;	Kyokka eidembe libawo ngoli nomukali eyasimbaa ...

Errand –

Compare the pschological time and space of the Chant above, with the pschological time and space of the text from Historical Africa archive **by Asar Imhotep as below –**

In Historical Africa archive, we see men and Womyn working together – as the picture here above shows off that while the man ploughs the woman; a co-worker on the Courtyard "home" and that is to say a wife is in no other place than to come along to saw! And that brings us to the point that a marriage is a very old thing – and it came about because of NOT Human labour exploitation as such BUT because of this notion of survival! The idea that; it is better to survive in company of a co-work than it is as an individual out in this life! So, living in union goes back to the time that we cannot even count ...

Sennedjem and his wife Iy-Neferti preparing fields in the afterlife.

Asar Imhotep 2016

... Now, it is within that context that we have marriage. That a wife or husband is supposed to be a co-worker. And so, you live this life and you aspire, or if you believe in Divine purpose, but you NEED unity along the way. Because the world is going to send challenges that are difficult to overcome by oneself. So, we unity with each other to make life easier. But not for the sake that one person does all the work while the other does little to nothing! Practically it does not make sense!

Quiz;

- How is HLPF planning for Africa Spoken Languages will tell Africa History properly **without Initiatives contributing to the implementation of the SDGs Count for Africa School Curriculum Reform 2022**

- We do remember that during the era of MDG2015 HLPF did not hesitate to find which MDGs to implement to solve the Africa phenomenon FGM. HLPF has enough resources for start-up phase for Africa School Curriculum Reform 2022.

Diop on the material factors and status of Egyptian women

In fact it is only in this framework that the wife can, in spite of her physical inferiority, contribute substantially to the economic life. She even becomes one of the stabilizing elements in her capacity as mistress of the house and keeper of the food.

C.A. Diop, *The Cultural Unity of Black Africa* (Chicago: Third World Press, 1990), 34.

"Diop, as above fig. when talking about Africa contexts, Diop talks of the material factors, that led to the elevation status of Womyn, in Kemet; ancient Africa compared to the Indo-European counterparts. Now we got to remember that Kemet for a greater part was an agrarian society in the same way Africa is agrarian society almost in all ways. Now, agrarian societies have developed over time through building differently from the pastoral/ nomadic societies that build over time from nomadic – pastoralism like the Proto Indo-European societies were. But can we agree more with Diop, where he describes a woman as a physical inferior body"? **Asar Imhotep**

"In Bugwere, a woman is super able body being transferred from one clan or folk group to another! That is how and where bride price comes in! in Bugwere a woman is super able body, that is why Bugwere Divination is commonly woman gender assignment. In Bugwere a woman is super body – to every Customary ceremony there is a clever old woman. But again, in Historical Africa Archive – where there is Asar there is Aset; where there is Djehuti there is Seshata – Now, in Bugwere where there is Ikumbania there is Itulula? In the Chant above, the bachelor admits he is strong but weakened because of living as a single able body. Then I think that Asar, Djehuti, Ikumbania etc. are complemented in the company of Aset, Seshata, Itulula etc. therefore, in the woman physical body, there must be an energy or something else that must be in place only if man and woman become co-workers". **Participant.**

Asar Imhotep; It is therefore no wonder that in Ancient Africa archive we find record reading – (" *Egyptian marriage; /grg pr/ – to found or establish our house in unity"*). For records, let you understand and know that; there was no such thing like marriage in Kemet; Ancient Africa as per the meaning of the Ranykemet word /grg pr/ means to found or establish our house in unity as earlier mentioned above. Alternatively – **see fig below here.**

Egyptian marriage

The Egyptians used the term, **grg pr**, which simply means to "found or establish your household", and a man and a woman became married by setting up a "house" **together.** (Allen, 2009: 29)

Dr. Troy Allen (mr-$hr.w$)

Asar Imhotep 2016

"If we travel back 2 – 4 generations we can recapture Bugwere courtyard or "home" – modern way of life of customary Africa courtyard. we will need to find a root e.g. "tree" for gender terms that mean a man/ a woman personal – human being BUT not just any personal human being, in terms of just the idea person. But, more so in active living body! And so, the root "tree" here also in Ranykemet language; mdw nTr – the first written down language in ancient Africa script kweke ↔ hm make notice that Kemet in ancient Africa did not write out their vowels. is one of the many living examples that we can use. So, this "hm" – dialectically when we go far back to Ranykemet language script the word "hm" is the root ward for "tree-branch". And from the root word "hm" comes a variety of ideas! And so, from this notion of Tree and tree-truck. Early man in Kemet came with the idea of comparing the human body to the tree; Tree ↔ body. And from there comes the concept of the human body. And so, in the second column we can place the concept of a King (male/ female). God (male/ female) etc. more so, where we talk in the context of the able body – the arm, which means power to do work! And from this notion of power to do work, is delivered the idea of service/ servant, craftsmen; or somebody in his/ her skill. A priest etc. is talking of the idea of man and Womyn in union. Something to make notice of is that in Ancient Africa children are born as either male or female. Therefore, must be educated into initiation to man – Women. A duty that was a signed to the Temples in the Valley of River Hapi (Nile)" **Asar Imhotep 2016**.

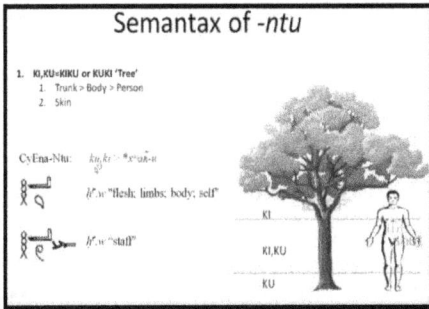

Semantax of -ntu

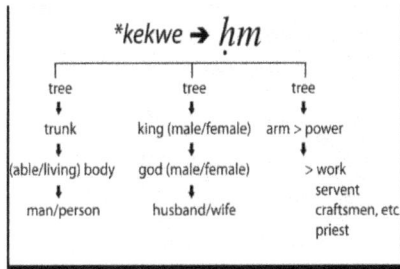

*kekwe → hm

tree	tree	tree
trunk	king (male/female)	arm > power
(able/living) body	god (male/female)	> work
man/person	husband/wife	servent
		craftsmen, etc.
		priest

Bugwere incentive Chants to Go back to School

A challenge in Bugwere Value; Thought and Did compare the two texts – one from Bugwere compared to Historical Africa text to follow below here –

Community-building;	Twali tutyaime nga tetumaitte, tuti'okusooma kuwoma inn
Participants;	Yelele maama, yele maama, yelele maama, yelele maama.

Community-building;	Ekyalo Bugwere munsii e nu Uganda, ensii' enu' nungi, tinjeru tukutuku atenga tiziggi ziggi.
Participants;	Yelele maama, yele maam, yelele maam, yelele maama

Errand;

Implementation of SDG4 quality education is "To make, prove to retrace one's steps, refer to place of origin; restore –

""Make secure, set right (a wrong), provide, fulfil, a contract"; "to restore, repair, to make new again" to make grow, flourish"" i.e. "future we want" **rebirth of knowledge**

Helping Africa States and Governments make implementation of Mother Language UNESCO-SDG4 quality education, is indicator Africa need School Core-Curriculum reform. If the United Nations; HLPF/ EASG June 2012 Resolutions; "future we want" … in the era of SDG4 mean good for Africa development, then it is high time for Africa School Curriculum reform. There are enough Educators who are standing strong for Africa History into Curriculum Books, let alone the Stakeholder who come up with inputs about SDG4 to the HLPF September 2019 The Origin of Africa Languages, Scientific Comparative Method book by Mboli; 2010 – "Well, this is syllabus Book for higher studies one may say". NONETHELESS, here this Project concerns itself about the culture of the Book – the culture in this book is firstly Africa even if the literature is Academic … if u see the point! The way AVwDHA and BCOR see it, the culture of this book is also useable in participatory information seminars. Moreover, if colonial languages are teachable from pre-primary schools to the highest level of education. Certainly, Mother Language Ranykemet is teachable in Africa from pre-primary to the highest education level. … That is what this Project idea brings to the table as far as Africa Spoken languages in rural Africa libraries and Africa School core-curriculum is concerned.

Chants of love from Bugwere

Compare modern love life with Love life in Ancient Africa to follow below –

Gasyoddo, wamaitte nga tontakka, lwakki wangabire ebulawuzzi yoo? Ebulawuzzi yo yandetere okulwalaaaa!

Wempere enu ebulawuzzi yange, nalyamu eyo e kikajjooo.

Lover;	Mboinne oKadondi no'mutinii.
Chorus;	Eehehe taile.
Lover;	Alin'e nziri gye kilalo.
Chorus;	Eehehe taile.
Lover;	Kaissi e langi ye kigowa.
Chorus;	Eehehe taileee.
Lover;	Tonkoberanga'omulodi wange.
Chorus;	Ali e Naboa'e yo mweru.
Lover;	Tonkoberanga'omulodi wange.
Chorus;	Ee eehe eehe taileeee.

Munange wamaitte nga tontakka, lwakki wangabire'o simoni woooo? O simoni wo yandetere okulwalaaaa!

Wempere enu osimoni wange, nalyamu eyo e kikajjooo.

Mboine'oNauddo no mutini. Eh eee eee talire

Tonkoberanga'omulodi wange, alye'e Naboa' yo mweruuu

Chants from mates to discipline the rude girl

Mates; Baala, baala, baala, bolingo
Participants; Baala musetuke tupakase o busweeti

Mates; Mwaala a tasanyukka nabainaye, yebulira.
Participants; Mwaala a tasanyukka nabainaye, a swazza.
Baala musetuke tupakase o busweeti ...

Chant of manhood to pursued community let him marry the girl of his dreams.

Leader;	Ohoooo o'mwaala'o gwe nkunga.
Chorus;	Namunaga bamuwaire'e kidda.
Leader;	Ohoooo naye nkole intya?
Chorus;	Namunaga bamuwaire'e kidda.

Errand;

The lover's mates will stand by their mate to chant every evening to beat the point into the Ears of the Community Elders.

Chant to sermon the dream girl −

The Mates;	Saala oooowe, Saala.
participsnts;	Abalungi mulumya, Saala.
The girls;	Onjetera nga niki Saala.
Participants;	Saala, abalungi balabye Saala
The mates;	Inkwetera musaizza, Saala.
Participants;	Abalungi mulumya, Sala.
The Mates;	Saala oooowe, Saala.
Participants;	Abalungi mulumya, Sala.
Saala;	Onjetera nga niki Saala.
Participants;	Sala, abalungi balabye Sala
The Mates;	Inkwetera musaizza, Saala.
Parcipanta;	Abalungi balabye, Saala.

Recall –

"What is love? Well, love is a verb, it is something that you practice! Love is not a feeling! Now, you better keep that in mind, Practice on the principles of Maat for strength" **Asar Imhotep**

Errand –

Initiative in contributing in implementation of SDGs … Coordinate related Projects to challenge an illuminate each other. Bugwere, 2022 visiting Linguistics should meet Bugwere lore on the local library books shelves not in participatory seminars Business as usual.

Chant of our everyday lives in Bugwere Community

Bugwere folklore Saaga; Value in Thought – Did

The Majority;	Oh koizeyo, koizeyo.
The Minority;	Koizeyo tuliyo
The Majority;	Oh koizeyo, koizeyo.
The minority;	Koizeyo tuliyo
The Majority;	Oh eyisaanyu, eisanyu.
The Minority;	Eyisanyu lya njitta
The Majority;	Ale mwisukeyo ebiseera ebyo.
The Minority;	Ummmm mwenna okutusabira.
The Majority;	Oh eyisaanyu, eisanyu.
The Minority;	Eyisanyu lya njitta
The Minority;	Nagabengaaa.
The Majority;	Owee
The Minority;	Nagabenga okezera.

The Majority;	Ntuka mubugeni, Ntuka mubugeni banange, ntuka mubugeni.
The Minority;	Nabagenga nga'okezera. Oyibireku enyuma
The Majority;	Ndi njibba kintu banange neyunna lugendo, o mwoyo gwagonere eyo nga gulota buloti!
The Minority;	Nabagenga okezera.
The Mojority;	Indi njibba kintu banange neyunna lugendo.
The Minority;	Mmmmmmmh
The Majority;	Akasana kanene, Mwena mukabone. Ebigere byange binnu tebitakka mwisana Mulimu'o buntu buddi'o mutakula'o mubigere.
The Minority;	Gaba ganfunzza?
The Majority;	Mmmmmmh o baire watukya. Mwizze mu ndole'aganfuzza gademba ganjitta.
The Minority;	Nagabengaaa, iwe olimunyommi. Ekintu ekyeikkaaa, iwe kyotta o mubugeni.
The Majority;	Munkubiremu ekyo, o munwa tilugalii, ebyo tubireke. O'nkoko waise o musesere, mwabe mulete. Ombuli waiswe owomulevu, yena babage.
The Minority;	Ummmmmmm
The Majority;	Omutwe, ebigere ebyo mudyakke.
The Minority; The Majority;	Onanyere e ika Yelire,

The Minority;	Onanyere e eika
The Verdict;	Yeliireeee, yeliiree, yeliireeeeeeeeeeeH

Moral -

Living in Society is like travelling on a Ship, everyone must put on a Helm. The same way, living in the era of Initiative Contribution to SDGs pschological Time and Space. Majority HLPF must include more minority Stakeholders and MGoS at the Important Decision-Making Desk ... **"future we want"**.

Chant of Jobseeker – Africa Value in Thought – Africa Value in Did

MWABBI

Mwabbi;	Ekkidda hooo, ekkidda hooo ekkidda hooo ekkidda!
Participants;	Ekkidda hooo, ekkidda hooo ekkidda hooo ekkidda!
Mwabbi;	Ekkidda banange e kkidda.
Participants;	Kidambirenge!
Mwabbi;	Ekkidda banange e kkidda.
Participants;	Kidambirenge!

Mwabbi;	Kiddima na munalire tobona, namunalire. Kiddima na munaliire o lwe kkidda.
	Aahaaa, aahaaa wululu, aahaa. Aahaaa mwe ndekere iimwe ii mbasaliza inno kirya ya mbulya nga o'luganjja o luunna lwakki?

Participants;	O luganjja o lubunna bwire nti olima?
Mwabbi;	Ekyo kifuffu e wange ingonna mubissoinggi?

Mwabbi;	Obwendima inyerengeta iino to bonna, inyerengeta iino, Obwendima iinyerengeta iino iiwee.
Participants;	Obwendima insukka mugaiga, tobonna – insukka mugaiga, obwendima insukka mu kombe imweeee
Mwabbi; Participants;	Ekkidda banange e kkidda. Kidambirenge!
Mwabbi; Participants;	Ekkidda banange e kkidda. Kidambirenge!
Mwabbi; Participants;	Omulaaloo aafera mukulisya egya yabba, Kidambirenge.
Mwabbi; Participants;	Enjjaggi a yekka ku yekka o lwekkidda. Kidambirenge.
Mwabbi; Participants;	Zzenna ndagga kudagga olwekidda. Kidambirenge.
Participants; Mwabbi;	Mwabbi aafera ku lyenggi egya jabba Kidambirenge
Participants; Mwabbi;	Kigonna a datta ku datta olwekidda. Kidambirenge.
Participants; wululu, aahaa. Mwabbi;	Zzenna ndagga kudagga olwekidda. Aahaaa, aahaaa Aahaaa, mwe ndekerenge immeeeeeeeeeeeeeeH

Moral –

Life in the Diaspora deserves safe return to Mother Land.

/Sm. m. Htp/ Kulwenzza-Otim …

Chant

Onyonyi mMutono Nzeremba carries political philosophy message –

Standby ... Onyonyi oMutono; oNzelemba Saaga – when communal wisdom blend in the meaning of hardworking

1. The majority; Onyonyo omutono.
   The Minority; Nzeremba, onyonyi, onyonyo omutono nzeremba.
   The majority: Onyonyo omutono.
   The Minority; Nzeremba, onyonyi, onyonyo omutono nzeremba.

2. The minority; Onyonyi oyooooooo.
   The Majority; Nzeremba, aaaaaaaaa, Nzeremba
   The Minority; Onkodoleeeeeeeeeeee.
   Participants; Nzeremba, aaaaaaaaa, Nzeremba.

3. The minority; Onyonyo omutono.
   Participants; Nzeremba, onyonyi, onyonyo omutono nzeremba.
   The minority: Onyonyo omutono.
   Participants; Nzeremba, onyonyi, onyonyo omutono nzeremba.

4. The majority; Ke kyussa kyussaaaaaaaaaaaaaaaaaa ...
   The minority; Nzeremba, onyonyi, omutono nzeremba.
   The majority; Ka sonya banna be.
   The Minority; Nzeremba, aaaaaaaaa, Nzeremba.

5. The majority; Ohhh, banange e kyenkoba.
   The minority; Hmmmmm.
   The majority; Twabe tu kalete.
   The minority; Hmmmmm.
   The Majority; kaisi tukadunde.
   The Minority; Hmmmmm.
   The Majority; Kaisi tukarile.
   The minority; Hmmmmm.

| The Majority; | Oku bwitta okuwoma. |
| The Minority; | Nzeremba |

6. The minority;   Oh Nzeremba, nzeremba aaaaaaaaa, Nzeremba.
    The majority;   Nzeremba, nzeremba aaaaaaa, nzeremba

    The minority;   Onkodoleeee, nzeremba aaaaaaa, nzeremba

    The majority;   Nzeremba aaaaaa nzeremba

7. The minority;   Onyonyo omutono.
    The Majority;   Nzeremba, onyonyi, omutono nzeremba.
    The minority;   Onyonyo omutono.
    The Mojority;   Nzeremba, onyonyi, omutono nzeremba.

8. The majority;   Onyonyo omutono.
    The Minority;   Nzeremba, onyonyi, omutono nzeremba.
    The majority;   Onyonyo omutono.
    The Minority;   Nzeremba, onyonyi, omutono nzeremba.

9. The majority;   Oooooo banange ekindi te.
    The minority;   Hmmmm.
    The majority;   Kawoma kokye.
    The minority;   Hmmmm.
    The majority;   Kaisi otumunyu
    The minority;   Hmmmm.
    The majority;   Okubwitta okuwoma.
10. The minority;   Oo'nzerembaa,
    The majority;   nzerembaa aaaaaa nzeremba.
    The minority;   Onyoyi ooyoooh,
    The majority;   Nzerembaa aaaaaaa nzeremba

11. The majority;   Onyonyo omutono.
    The minority;   Nzeremba, onyonyi, omutono nzeremba.
    The majority: Onyonyo omutono.
    The minority;   Nzeremba, onyonyi, omutono nzeremba.

12. The majority;   Onanyere eika,
    The minority;   Yelilre eeeee yelire
    The majority;   Onanyere eika,
    The minority;   Yelilre eeeee yelire

13. The minority;   Onyonyi oyooooooo.
    The majority;   Nzeremba, aaaaaaaaa, Nzeremba
    The minority;   Onkodoleeeeeeeeeeee.
    The majority;   Nzeremba, aaaaaaaaa, Nzeremba.
    The minority;   Ooo...nyonyi ... oyooooooo.
    The Verdict;   Nzerembaaaaaa haaaaa. Nzerembaaaaaaaaaah.

From the Chant; "*Onyonyi'omutono*"and as above here, Bugwere lore prompt to –

The charm of "living in society"; for both the Minority and the Majority should listen, challenge and illuminate each other. In this Chant replace "the Majority" with "our political lives" consequently, replace "the Minority" with "our everyday lives" to catch-up with Bugwere philosophizing.

Errand -

Put on a helm, contribute in the SDGs, Corruption is persistent when one group is left to make important decisions without the other ... so, go become a Stakeholder; actively contribute to SDGs ... "future we want" HPLF alone cannot make important decisions without challenge and illuminate of both minority and majority.

Quiz;
How does 996234843-AVwDHA.Org and Partner BCOR Pilot the research questions and their Assumption?

Chapter 4.

Methodology

Every educated or person can claim to know what is called a library, or art gallery and museum nonetheless, if truth be told; such buildings are meaningless to modern African until Africa Spoken languages union with Mother Language in Antiquity are studied and written down by Africa people themselves. Africa literature has been excluded from school core-curriculum the last 3 100 years. 1974 Diop and Obenga put on a massive debate in UNESCO-Cairo Conference to query the whereabouts of Africa History in Core-Curriculum Books!

In the Era of SDG4 quality education for all input from Stakeholders to the High Level Political Forum Added Value is what Africa needs to do by the 2022 same question; what is your excuse? what is the excuse, not to introduce into school core-curriculum – Africa spoken languages reunion with Mother Language in Antiquity? The enough Seshew mdw nTr educators to begin to teach Ranykemet in Africa.

Identified research question 1.

Africa is home to a diversity of Spoken Languages; Africa image is no longer visible due to too much corruption. The money mongers can overrun this Project Idea; the Principle of Building Local Libraries in Rural Africa take over the idea, set-up buildings named local libraries undermining the principles of building local libraries in rural Africa, how can we trust in the 21st. century something important like this Project Idea will work in Africa for Africa?

Assumption 1.

Three is greater than two. Whereby, the Stakeholders comes as number one. Africa States and Governments come out as number two. And the HLPF/ EASG come to make three. If the three come to table to challenge and illuminate each other. That way Corruption is left with no breathing space. Therefore, corruption goes away. If you see the point.

Assumption 2.

Corruption is not a Culture of Africa; corruption and racism come to Africa embedded in invented traditions. Also commonly known as development aid to Africa. Corruption if those with knowledge of a shareable good insist on development aid without School Curriculum Reform! That is corruption.

It is wise for Africa, you and I to pay attention to Eric Hobsbawm and Terence Ranger PDF 1983 – "inversion of traditions is the use of ancient materials to construct invented traditions of a novel type for quite a novel purpose. A large store of such materials is accumulated in the past in any ancient society and an elaborated language of symbolic practice and communication is always available. Sometimes new traditions could be readily grafted on old ones. Sometimes they could be devised by borrowing from the well supplied warehouses of official ritual symbolism and moral exhortation – religious and princely pomp, folklore and freemasonry (itself an earlier invented tradition of Great Symbolic Force) ... **Eric Hobsbawm and Terrance Ranger PDF 1983"**;

Identified research question 2.

How does AVwDHA/ BCOR Participatory Information Seminar Project; Pilot the research questions?

Assumption 3.   It shouldn't be the job of AVwDHA/ BCOR Participatory Information Seminar Project; to pilot the research question. The research questions should unfold from the participants in the information seminars. The best things AVwDHA/ BCOR have discovered under the seminars is why and how it matters to building local Libraries in rural Africa. The second is the implementation of SDG4 quality education must be in favour of Africa School Curriculum reform to foster Africa spoken languages reunion with mother language in Antiquity and in turn to foster the local library in community.

I know you know this makes sense.

Research question 3.

Can the Project Idea; Building local libraries in rural Africa create job opportunities in Rural Africa?

Assumption 4.

Yes, and we are talking of quality jobs. And that includes "how and why" the Principle of building libraries in rural Africa matters. Which again point out that "future we want" – the School Core-Curriculum Reform foster the Principles of

Building Library, an Art Gallery, Museum in rural Africa. further to that, in the 21st. century, the building of local library, Art and Craft Galleries, Museum etc. in rural Africa should complement each other with go back to school and create quality jobs.

Assumption 5	Africa must be helped to adopt to the culture of language Comparative Method whether by available methodology to restore Africa Spoken languages reunion with Mother Language in antiquity in a conscious way. Let the Mother Language Ranykemet be taught in Africa from pre-primary to highest level of education then the daughter languages automatically will find their place in Ranykemet; the Mother Language Knee. Ranykemet is Africa Mother Language in Archive i.e. Negro Egyptian language as she evolves in Psychological Time and Space ... Knowledge of Ranykemet Language in Africa will stabilize Africa people. Africa people reciting at the living Oral Literature in a conscious way is "future we want".

The problem is if you are going to tell Africa History properly, you are going to get a big problem with from the authors of "invented traditions! All of them; the Missionaries, Colonialism, the current development aid of educate to Africa, have the same goal; to disorient modern Africa from her History. Now if you are going to look History of Africa right in the eye, you are going to get a black eye. It is important to know why True Africa Educators and Leaders get boxed in a corner and silenced. Now the World is taken into a psychological problem! Development aid is embedded with invented traditions, racism and corruption and the world is coerced to consume development aid whole package as it is.

/Sm. m. Htp/ Kulwenzza-Otim in the Diaspora you did your Initiative in contributing to the era of SDG Pschological Time and Space.

Chapter 5.

Findings/ Results –

The Project Idea findings reveal that in folklore lies a Fountain of value in thought – did condensed in Spoken Languages. The Objective of this research is to Challenge and illuminate in both our everyday lives as well as in our HLPF lives. The suggested challenge for year 2022 is fierce, but the courage, the incentive to go on lies in initiative in "future we want" … in the coming HLPF meeting September 2019 under the unfolding implementation of Mother Language UNESCO-SDG4 quality education for Africa adds up to School Curriculum Reform in Africa if not everywhere. To foster Africa Spoken Languages reunion with Mother Language in Antiquity. To foster the Principles of Building Local Libraries in Rural Africa.

The Introduction, the Context, the Gathered Lore, the Methodology etc. challenge the HLPF lazy formulation of Implementation of SDG4 quality education. HLPF must emphasize the point; Living no one behind cannot be if a people cannot define word used in spoken language on Mother Knee with reference to Mother Language in antiquity. Here is the scenario, there is wisdom in Building Libraries in Rural Africa based on Principles put on the HLPF decision making desk. So that by year 2022 the start-up phase in School Core-Curriculum Reform in Africa is in place. So that he or she who wants to enter to live, work or research in Africa must come with a certificate in at least sSw mdw nTr – scribe in Ranykemet the surviving mother language of Africa Spoken Languages studying Africa lore based on language comparative method. Moreover, there are four identified words in the literature that are going to be examined and analysed in this Chapter 5. The core of Chapter 5 in this social research is "word study" Starting with the word "Saaga" is found in more than one spoken language, in our pschological time and places. Most of all the word can function in the same way regardless of which language of choice. Take for example in both Lugwere language spoken in Eastern Uganda and Norwegian Language, an Indo-European language spoken in Scandinavia, the word Saaga or Saga function in the same way. This is opportunity to make a step to analyse/ examine this word plus three more; (Saaga, Gweere, eimerera "Libation Pour" and Kirolero) are the few identified words from the participatory seminar; Chapter 3; gathering Bugwere Lore, written literature and Authors to consider on this round. Given the lore/ text relation in chapter 3. Above, the Information Seminar in Sensitizing in Bugwere proves able to relate to how and why "*word phenomenon must be studied and analysed in relationship to psychological time and space".* From what we learn from chapter 3; the Lore/ text "words" match the psychological time both in Africa Spoken Languages union with Mother Language in Antiquity?

An analysis in chapter 3 exemplify how "the Principles of Building Local Libraries in Rural Africa" take root from implementation of SDG4 quality education – Africa School Curriculum Reform to foster Africa Spoken Languages reunion with Mother Language in Antiquity. To foster the Principles of building local libraries in rural Africa. Studying Africa words will befit Africa.

Chapter 3. Brings on some Authors/ linguistic in verdict. Chapter 3; Aim at causing awareness – firstly; why we shouldn't give a blind eye to language comparative method. Secondly, this social research is initiative in contributing to SDGs – "future we want" Meaning that a language or a Nation in African who have written down Africa spoken languages independent of comparative method, risks to marginalize the language in question. Thirdly, Building Local Libraries in Rural Africa on Established Principles is going to foster Creation of Quality Jobs. Being conscious of such questions and more leads us to sure knowledge Africa must build local libraries on which Principles. Adding up to the several reasons for advocacy of the implementation of Mother Language-UNESCO-SDG4 quality education in favour of Africa spoken languages union with mother language, foster creating quality jobs etc.

Results

In Lugwere language it is almost unusual for words to function independent of a prefix or suffix. Like it is said, Africa Languages are Oral literature, when this is the case, in Lugwere Language the word "Saaga" is a muffin/word used to describe the act of "joking". But Not only, the word Saaga also is used to describe the act of searching for news or search from history. Here we know this conversation is not about "the verb to joking". Here we know this conversation is about the verb "looking for or searching". So, Bagwere following this conversation, can easily identify that this conversation is heading to the verb "looking/ searching" for someone or something. Which means the seminar intends to tell the audience to look/ search for information from Bugwere language. In this regard, using the word Saaga in Lugwere language, the sentence can look or sound like one of the following; notice that in the word/ muffin "Saaga" letter "g" is interchangeable with letter "k" then the same word can be spelt either as "Saaga" or "Saaka".

Omulutumo oLugwere –

- "Ndikusaagamu mungelo gyo lutumo olwaiswe". **Meaning; I am doing a search in Lugwere lore**
- "Twaabe enzza tusaake amayaka". **Meaning; let us go out to look/ search for news etc.**

It is interesting to find this same word in Indo-European language Norwegian use the word saaga as above. But I do not think in Norwegian language the word Saga has other functions other than the search function.

The word "Gweere"

The word Gweere is a muffin word in Lugwere language. This same word functions in three different ways by putting on prefix or suffix, see below.

- "Abagweere ba Bagweere". **Meaning Bagwere have been invaded**
- Ondekke emeere engweere". **Meaning please, let me eat my meal in peace.**
- "Abagweere bataka beBugwere". **Meaning invaders are the natives in Bugwere.**

The word "Gweere"

This muffin courses some disturbance. Examining the word "Gweere" challenges Bugwere not to overlook the fact that Bugwere people have a job to do with regards, word function. But again, this should Prompt Bugwere to Add Value to Lugwere language by building a local library where Bagwere will go to Study Lugwere Language, which means that the people consciously gain knowledge of the local spoken language.

The word "Kirolero"

Notice that in Bantu languages letter "L" and letter "R" are interchangeable in the same position. So, in the word Kirolero, letters "R" and "L" can be in either positions.

In our seminar we find that the word Kirolero" is composed of two words. Because "Kiro" is prefix on the muffin word "ilore".

"ilore" in Lugwere Language means the animalia body part "eye" or an object used for viewing.

"malore" in Lugwere Language is either

(a) Eye – singular = ilore and the plural = malore+lo, or
(b) Eye disease

Lugwere sentences using the muffin "malore"

- Obulamalorelo? Meaning; don't you have eyes?
- Alinamalore; meaning the person in question is suffering from eye disease

"Kirolero" is a word or name that was Perhaps created from association of body parts and ideas;

In Chapter 6. Under the workshop, the seminar will show-off with "Association of Ideas," from comparative method by Jean Claude Mboli 2010 and Asar Imhotep.

Here, the Lugwere word/ Phrase "Kirolero" is the name or word used to describe the house where a Clan or Courtyard holds meetings, a dining room, a place to host visitor or Collars on mediation mission. Mind you the place or house Kirolero can never be used for sleeping house/ place.

Now, if we analyze the word Kirolero, it is possible that ...

Literary, the Lugwere word "Kirolero" is **association of ideas** to describe an object or place/ house where Important Decisions Are Made in Bugwere. Kirolero is Bugwere associate of ideas; looking into matter at a higher level, examining phenomenon, analyzing information at a higher level etc. as we shall show-off in the Workshop chapter 6.

Quiz

Where else in Africa can we find houses of Kirolero category, to compare with to prove what we argue here, what or which details shall we be looking for etc.

- "Amasaabo" of Obuganda people.
- "Togu na" house of words in Dogon people of West Africa
- "Kgotla" customary court of Botswana people and loanword lekgotla in South Africa
- Temples in Ancient Africa.

Now, if the identified words or names to the houses (Amasabbo, Togu na, Kgotla, Temples) from around Africa match Bugwere house "Kirolero". The signs to look for will be

- The house itself must have several entre, must be door less.
- Central figures e.g. Deity, Diviner, Judge, Griot etc.
- Dress Code.
- Rules of procedure.
- Recitation/ prayer at the commencement of any meeting.
- Libation Pour.

The word eimerela –

To analyze the word eimerela requires a course of 14 – 16 weeks.

Customary, the word "eimerela" is word of blessing, a recitation/ prayer a Ritual led by a Deity. When the deity mention of the word eimerela, Libation Pour is along with. the Deity mentions the word four time and in between, the Deity performs Libation Pour before the mention of the word eimerela a gain.

Namaddu

Namaddu Custom takes place on Call/ order from Kirolero. The same applies to the performance of Libation Pour then recitation at "eimerela" comes with.

This seminar brought this up to inspire the reader, understand that – it is in the nature of Oral literature to condense many words and did in just a muffin of a word or Did ... such that it is tempting to conclude that; the reason why Deveiners spit on a charm/ herb before handing over to the Caller is because of the way of Oral literature condensing many ritual into small space of a word muffin or simple Did. When the deveiners spits on a charm – it could be in Libation Pour replacement.

Asar Imhotep; We keep not thousands of words of which we will not remember. We keep a few words which we can combine and expand when discussing different aspects of reality.

Mboli brings this out in his research in Kemet in Ancient Africa language reconstruction for example the word *"ka -ø or KA for stick"* in Ancient Africa that would be *"ke for thing"* but the determinative still has stick. The challenge in studying Ranykemet language; the first written down language in ancient Africa is that they did not write down their vowels. And so, how do you know what the word is talking about when the script reveals only consonants. Well, they put pictures of the thing being talked about. Or it was an idea, they would put a papyrus rope to indicate thinking man. If it was water/ a river or whatever they would put a determinative at the end of the word, that concedes with the fundamental word itself. For example, the first word ka or ki for stick becomes a word for an object but then it has an expanded meaning for tool, a thing, and then it becomes a secondary semantic word for hard, force, dangerous, stone. You know always referring to its fundamental. This word "ku, for foot, tree, place to be. Ultimately is where we get the word garb - in earth, and Igbo (the Igbo people) which means forest. But this word (garb- is Ancient Egyptian comes from the word ku/b word), becomes rounded and turns into "W" and that how the word turns into garb/earth same word for foot, is the same word for place, earth, and base. This is where we get the word ma 'at! Because you see the word ma 'at is with meaning foot, base. And the word KMT itself. Again, this is another word whose meaning we R still struggling with; some scholars argue the word KMT means black but with this comparative method we find that KMT means place, foot, base, ground. But, the way KMT teaches the human body is the base of the grammar of our languages, so the way KMT so it, they related everything to foot, which is also the tree! So, Asar Imhotep has also come up with the hypothesis that from evolution standpoint; the tree as it shows here is coming from the forest, this is how we came out of the forest. because tree is our life. And so, we going to relate everything to it.

Mboli 2010

Mboli 2010 argues that the majority words of the Negro Egyptian come from the world tree! And we should understand how worlds are built. You see, for us oral literature people. Our strong side is we are handy – we are quick to trust; we do not cherish in collecting words and keep unnecessary! So, we keep just enough. Same thing really when it comes to word development, we do not need to have a lot of words. Oral Literature keeps a few words which can be used to combine in various ways to suite the subject matter. Occasionally, musicians also act this way. In this literature we have seen that the words "Saaga/ Saaka", the word "Gweere", the word "irole" etc. function in several ways.

Go support Africa Build Local Libraries in Rural Africa to foster Africa spoken Language reunion with Mother Language in Antiquity.

Chapter 6.

Discussion/ Workshop –

Summary of how Africa Spoken languages (see diagram of Mboli 2010) have evolved with Early man in Antiquity. Remember this information is based and extract from the Book Title; Comparative Method written by Jean Claude Mboli 2010. Then later we will base on this diagram to practice on Sound Law as Africa scholar try to connect to Africa in the Past –

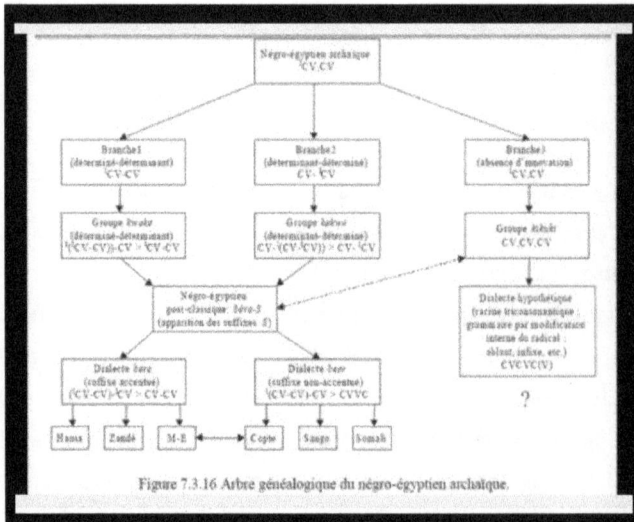

Figure 7.3.16 Arbre généalogique du négro-égyptien archaïque.

We need to bring out visual aid to how possibly spoken languages have evolved over time. So bear with this information seminar for bringing out a chart from the methodology book; comparative method – Jean Claude Mboli 2010 says in his methodology that; from his research, he discovered therefore puts forward his argument that Negro Egyptian language family developed as a result of extrusion of the word or vocabulary two different methods for formulating words of which he Mboli describes as; **"Kekwe or kweke"** these are same word, however, the syllables are switched in the case of the first word **"Kekwe"** and then into the other "**kweke**" and then, as a result of the convergence in history migrating groups ...

The Chores/ Errands/ Tasks

Here it is wise for the seminar presenter to present the self with a short family background. Take for example the book writer will go ahead and present herself briefly. By saying; maiden name is; Naikambo, born and raised in Bugwere, born in Basiikwe Clan, on Nadongha Courtyard, Kamonkoli - Nyanzza village. Twezzuma Bwiisonkere. Naikambo is now a mother, grandmother Community-worker and Book writer.

Hand out the presentation forms, the Chores, Errand and Material Pamphlet at the beginning of the seminar and collect the forms at the end of the seminar.

Suggest what to expect on the next seminar

Every new stage is advancement to course awareness about the missing links to Africa History.

Partisipants Evaluation form

Ciimelera, eiimelera no lusaagalukko omuunsli ya Kimbumba

- Aa malina go ...
- E 'itamba ....
  - o (GUEST in case someone is just visiting, write guest)

- Ee kiikka tuli ....   Twezuma ...
- Olugga lwa Mukulu ......
- Ekyalo ......
- Embugga

Date; ....Seminar at   ...... Oitekekku ekinkumu   .... oba omukono gwo

Participants be humbled. Accept to fill out the form to write correct information and write neatly because, there forms will remain kept and will go down in record! With these seminars, we are assembling structures and development on which Bugwere Libraries, Museums, and Gallery stand consequently Bugwere Local History.

If this native community; Bugwere is to build and keep a library or Museums. These must be based on what Bugwere have done in History and by filling these forms u R History in the making ... Importantly is for u to ask yourself; how do I want to be remembered in Bugwere History and Development.

There will be premier to the winners. The premier will come from your personal photographs previously taken by BCOR at your home with your loved ones reciting at folklore, a song, a folk-dance or simply a native short story of inspiration. We tailor this for you into a book. One copy to Bugwere Library and another copy for you to keep, forever. Every year should present a seminar or two or more depending on the response from Bugwere and the resources at hand and the response from those who want to advance to Africa history studies, Uganda authority not least the United Nations HLPF/ EASG – June 2012 resolutions; "future we want".

Chores;   What is first spoken language on your Mother Knee?

Is there need of local Libraries, Museums, Art galleries to be present in your native community?

Who should build local library in your local community? Your mother language is your Heritage, would you like to prove it to the global society yourself?

N-E built from 10 onomatopoeic roots

- *ka « sound of dry wood being cut, sound of cracking a dry branch »,
- *hu « action of blowing, breath »,
- *tʷi « sound of the mouth trying to chew »,
- *hũ « action of smell, sniff »,
- *xu « sound emitted from the throat »,
- *ŋə « baby sound identified as call to his mother »,
- *kʷi « cry of shivering, to thrill »,
- *i « indication of remoteness, there »,
- *u « indication of proximity, here »
- *a « indication of size (big), indication of far away »

Asar Imhotep

This is a slide of the 10 onomatopoeia root words that Mboli has reconstructed in his analysis; this seminar brings the above fig to inspire people to go back to school. But before we go back to school, let us become familiar with Africa in Antiquity brought to the seminar from Mboli via Asar Imhotep; from where language developed.

- "ka – the sound of dry wood being cut and cracking off the branch.
- "hu – the action of blowing and breath

Spirit and breath

Jaba	*hyong*	"spirit"
Twi	*honhom*	"spirit"
Yoruba	*hon (oorun)*	"snore"
Yoruba	*ohùn*	"voice" (breath of life)
Hebrew	*hamah*	"to roar" (like waves)
Arabic	*hamhama*	"to mutter"
M-E	*hn*	"shout, cheering"
M-E	*hnhn*	"soft words, lullaby, songs"
M-E	*hn*	"thorax"
		(controls breath/chest area)

Asar Imhotep 2016

Chores;   Write down some basic word from your native language; these basic words comprise of the body parts (see fig; evolution of -Ntu part II below) and words corresponding to the English words liver, a person, people etc. compare with the other languages (see table above – the word for breath, spirit). Compare these words with your first spoken language on the mother's knee. Take just enough words as there is time for/ during the seminar. Otherwise we can arrange another seminar if the participants have need for it. The results we are looking for inspire school goers about paying attention to Africa History which has all along pulled out of school curriculum or as this Project Saga mother language. Not least, write down your native language words related to a personal belonging, words related to society chiefery. Importantly; tell a mythology of your native language about native land and her people.

Semantax of -*ntu*

1. **KI,KU=KIKU or KUKI 'Tree'**
   1. Trunk > Body > Person
   2. Skin

CyEna-Ntu: *ku,ki > *x'as-n*

   hʷ.w "flesh; limbs; body; self"

   hʷ.w "staff"

KI

KI,KU

KU

Fill in the presenters/ participants' form to endorse that you are ready to be one of the corner stones to the home library, museum art and gallery of your native language.

Errands;   Whether the seminar goes on orally or in script, please keep on writing down these words, and later ask your friends to tell you what these words are called in their mother language(s)

Errands;   Seminar leader work hand in hand with the local authority to make sure that before you conduct any seminar of this project, you get a letter of permission and rental security cabinct to store the peoples' local Library assets and liabilities.

Spirit and breath

Yoruba	*emí*	"spirit"
Yoruba	*èémí*	"breath"
Yoruba	*mí*	"breathe"
Igbo	*mmuọ*	"spirit"
Ga	*mumọ*	"spirit"
M-E	*ꜥm*	"breathe in"
Tshiluba:	*nnyumà*	"spirit"
Tshiluba:	*anyìmà*	"soul"

MATERIALS;   This is a method book prepared for Information Seminars in spoken languages - folklore Saaga reunion with Africa Mother Language in Antiquity.

Information Seminar are to be understood as sensitization material and inspiration to go back to school.

BCOR is simply a sensitization unit not Educator. BCOR can recommend where to purchase scholastic material for self-studies. Nonetheless, we must stand together with Africa States and Governments to query the United Nations; HLPF/ EASG June 2012 resolution – "future we want" Africa Spoken Language union with Mother Language in Antiquity and into School Core-Curriculum.

Query the United Nations; HLPF/ EASG by 2022 he or she who wants to enter to live, work and research in Africa must have at least a certificate in the introduction to Ranykemet the first written down language in Antiquity.

Tasks/ Your remarks;

- Was this general course worth your quality time?
- Was the course informative?
- In future, and that is, as from tomorrow, what will be your reason to come back for general knowledge of Africa mother language informative?

Workshop

Write down the words of your native language corresponding to the English words you see in the diagrams here. Write down your native language words related to person, society chiefery and tell a mythology of your native language about land and her people.

- Therefore, let us advocate for knowledge to understanding so that rural Africa is updated on what a public library, a museum and an art gallery stands for firstly; native history.

  - The Diagrams here below have been extracted from syllabus books during self-studies. Purposely to serve as visual aid in comparison between Africa Spoken Languages union with Mother Language in Antiquity. the example below here –

  - Start by posing the Q; who are the native people on this heredity land? What is the name of the spoken native language there?

  - These Qs are important because Bugwere like any society has hunger for light of knowledge and development. The only way to support a

community into development is by active participating without hiding
their place of origin.

Etymology of "spirit"

- Animating force
- Breath/breathe
- Wind; to blow
- Life
- Disposition, character; high spirit, vigor,
  courage; pride, arrogance

• Urhobo	*erhi*	"spirit double"
• Arabic	*riyh*	"spirit, wind"
• Hebrew	*ru*ʷ*ah, ru*ʷ*h-*	"spirit, wind, temper"
• Hebrew	*reyah*	"scent"
• Yoruba	*ori*	"luck, destiny"
Yoruba	*ori*	"spirit double"
• Lugbara	*ori*	"ghost"
Lugbara	*ori-ndi*	"soul"
• Swahili	*roho*	"spirit, soul"
• Kikuyu	*roho*	"spirit"
• Bantu:	*ribo*	"spirit" (123, 189)
• Bantu:	*rima*	"chest" (46, 80)
Bantu:	*rima*	"heart, soul, spirit" (123, 189)
Bantu:	*rimo*	"soul, spirit" (23, 189)
• Bantu:	*rumu*	"soul, spirit" (123, 190)
• Bantu:	*rumu*	"ghost, devil" (51, 99)
• Bantu:	*roho*	"spirit, soul" (123, 191)

$K\mathit{3}$ and Paronymy

- $k\mathit{3}w\mathit{t}$ "to carry, to support"
- $k\mathit{3}.t$ "thought"
- $k\mathit{3}.j$ "to think about, plot"
- $k\mathit{3}$ "soul, spirit, personality, essence"
- $k\mathit{3}$ "to say"

1. Word order/ Grammar how does Lugwere language order her language
   a. e.g. father has come home = V. S. O.; Verb Subject Object or otherwise?
2. Language stages
3. Vocabulary i.e. very difficult to substitute once learnt in child up bring

   e.g. head mouth ... about 100 basic words that have been collected by Africa Linguistics as basic to follow when we compare language context.

In the era of SDGs Pschological Time and Space Call is for –

- To make, prove to retrace one's steps, refer to place of origin; restore
  –
- "Make secure, set right (a wrong), provide, fulfil, a contract";
- "to restore, repair, to make new again" to make grow, flourish".

Recall –

In modern life, skills or education begins right from birth on a Mother's Knee. Later in life, we SHOULD do advanced education to cause progress and prosperity! For example, no one is born Man or Womyn! Culturally speaking, one is born either as female or male until she or he reaches that initiation age through either traditional home schooling or through the National Education System and studies then one is qualified as Man or Womyn – meaning; be prepared to become Womyn or man, the able bodies to nature off springs and society at large i.e. "I am because you are, you are because I am..."

Africa Spoken Languages on Mother's Knee

On the right-hand side on the figure below is how our ancestors in Kemet stored written sound law. They wrote down consonants minus vowels.

- Technically you can consider all languages come out of Africa languages! – it can be proven mathematically/ scientifically. However, there is a distinction, and that is the concept known as semantics – and it is the way people psychological map and see the universe, and then map it into a language culture. Cultures outside Africa may have the same technical terms as we do! But, approach to understanding the phenomena is what is different! Because of the region and history, they may particularly have. Take an example from the word (Sound of the Spirits) "to receive" – is not the same for Europeans and Africa

Lexeme	Hieroglyph	Meaning
mḥ		care
mḥj		to care for; to be concerned about
mḥj		A priest
mḥ.y		guardian
mḥ.w		Hunter; fish spearer

Let us make notice also that the (kweke ↔ hm) can be inversed. To give us that semantic slightly different shading; you know on that common theme of being able to work or being able to do. So, in that context you have the syllable switched so that "instead of hm – you have mh). So, on the chart as above you can see the meaning of mh as to care for, to be concerned etc. a priest is somebody who takes care of and is skilled in a certain nature. A guardian is in the same context because they observe and take care of folks. And so, in the context of guardian we have nurses, Doctors, teachers etc. and because that same root is built on this notion of skillset, we have this one to *mhw*, meaning hunter, fisher, gatherer etc. so all these ideas are built on the same root, same thing.

This another example given by linguistics about the same root word in cijLuba lexeme e.g. *mu.kubi* meaning; "priest" coming from the root kuba – meaning protected, or take care of or ensurering … and you see the word *mhy* meaning guardian. These are same word only in Egyptian language. And again, we see that *mhy* in Egyptian when inversed with a ("t"- sephix) we have the word support or a post in Lugwere is what we know as "mpango/ mpagi". We are shown this determinative at the bottom a tree branch and a club on the left – is determinative of a tree truck just like support in home, house - in its nature it symbolically meaning of support. In the same context of care, protection guardian and all things of that nature. We have also another root at the bottom for "give protection; defend". Then we can say for sure that mh and hm are the same semantic words for care, guardian, and protection.

Africa association of ideas with body parts; basing on "Comparative Method"; conversation with Mboli 2010"

Languages change all the time. Language is not static. However, languages do not change randomly! They follow a set of laws of sound. Jean -Claude Mboli 2010, therefore argued; Comparative method is the path to restore History and to prove that two languages are genetically related or not. The linguistics of the African History is very complex, and very long in time. Compared to other linguistics. for example, Indo-European, etc. Therefore, u need to tighten the comparative method to make genuine results. Genuine results are what we need to deliver from new comparative methods. This is How to read languages to prove if they are genetically related or not. So, If, one wants to establish that the few selected languages are genetically related! comparative method is the best method to apply in this case. So, by the means of Homonymy, association of ideas; where Africa stands in the History of man and his Negro Egyptians language, Ancient Africa came to create new concepts, and new ideas and many of these ideas are still in use the World today. This is so because the Homonymy of African languages. For example, the word Kongo from the Kingdom of Kongo is a complete counter part of the concept KMT. Because this muffin "NGO" sound, is equivalent to letter "m" in the final position or none final position; (please navigate the chart to and learn better) linguistically speaking. Phonetically speaking. Because, in Bantu speaking where we find "ngo", it is "m" in Egyptian language. Prof. Mubabinge Bilolo has established and illustrated that "k" which is prefixed in Kongo word, is equivalent to "t" in KMT, final position in Egyptian. But u cannot see that because of Homonymy between the word source "NGO"; (please navigate the chart at bottom left) "Ngolo" meaning Force, "ngo" meaning leopard, and "Sango" meaning Priest...

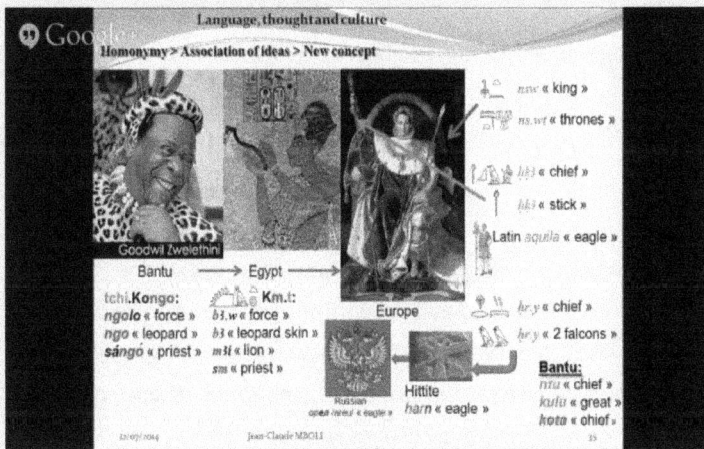

Mboli 2010"

The word also meaning; King Force but also magical force. In the pschological time and space of Africa in Kemet; is where the use of leopard skin dates from. It expresses force of the meaning of the word in Verdict. And, when the King wears a leopard skin, it means he is the Source! Basic of Bantu thinking! Any Bantu ceremony will have this leopard skin. So, this is ceremonial expression in Bantu languages without going in another language branch to explain this.

The custom occurred in pschological time and space in Ancient Africa as rule itself". The same custom occurs in pschological time and space in modern Africa. It does not need outsiders to explain these behaviours. Because we find this word called "*Bau*"; magical force and we find also this word leopard skin "*bau*". Bantu themselves will tell the difference. And there is another difficulty; why it is that when there is ceremony of Africa Royalty the Royals must be on the Royal throne? ...But when it comes to the Royals outside Africa and the way of Free Mesons outside Africa. They copy what was purely African creativity, they copy cuts and wear the Africa wears, let alone, up to present day, the Neo Indo-European hegemonies copy and wear like this, but they cannot explain this! This is purely "invented traditions" from Africa. On this notice, please refer to Eric Hobsbawm and Terrance Ranger PDF 1983 earlier mentioned ...

Recall

Association of ideas in Chapter 5 – when this seminar attempted to examine the word "Kirolero" the word application, the word association. The word proves to be associated with the body part - the "eye" idea. Let us say that is how and where Bugwere comes up with word "Kirolero" a name given to the said house. And as comparative method book by Mboli 2010 teaches that Spoken Languages were born from a mother language – studying Sound Law. Languages evolve maintaining the Pattern of association of ides. The seminar assumes Bugwere in Uganda – Africa likewise are capable of association of ideas to body parts mechanism following the Ranykemet pattern of the first true words as below –

Emergence of spoken language

First true words

1. **K+ø=KA 'Stick':**
   1. Object > Tool, Thing
   2. Hard > Force > Hurt, Dangerous, stone

2. **K+U=KU 'Tree' (lower part)**
   1. Foot > Place > To be
   2. Ground > Earth

3. **K+I=KI 'Tree' (upper part) > 'Branch'**
   1. Limb > Arm > To take; Horn, Tail
   2. Medicine

4. **KI,KU=KIKU or KUKI 'Tree'**
   1. Trunk > Body > person
   2. Skin

5. **KI,KU=KIKU or KUKI 'High place'**
   1. Head > Sky
   2. Mountain > Huge

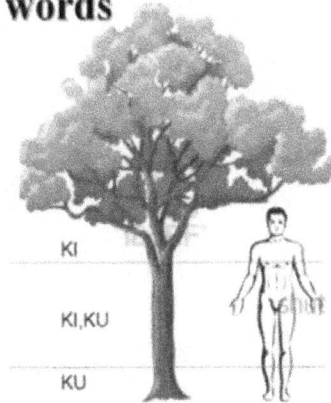

KI

KI,KU

KU

© Jean-Claude MBOLI   11/28/2015

From conversation with Mboli 2010 peer video;

- Ki = high-level or head of, force; (page 69 above)
- Ku = base-level or foot of a tree/ a place to be for example Home is a place to be.
-

In Lugwere Language – the word "kulugga" or to say "ndi wokulugga = this is my home; this is my base!

In chapter 5 we observed that "Kirolero" is Literary, the Lugwere word **association of ideas** to describe an object or place/ house where Important Decisions Are Made in Bugwere.

In the word Kirolero – "ki" is prefix = high level, and so is the body part/ organ "eye"

We know that looking into matters, is = high level, head, force etc.

So, we can see that Bugwere associate of ideas; looking into matter at a high-level, examining phenomenon, analyzing information is = to high-level etc.

Now, if we compare the prefix of the word Kirolero or muffin word "kiro" (recall in Bantu languages the "L" and letter "R" are interchangeable in the same word).

The fig. above prove that the "muffin" "ki" represents = high-level or Tool while "ku" = lower or foot or base – place to be **(look at the figure above page 88 and compare with the figure here below)**

The fig above, the muffin word Ki is associated with = head

The fig below, the muffin word ku is associated with = a foot, a path/ road.

Perhaps "Kirolero" is Bugwere associate of ideas; looking into matters calls for high level, examining phenomenon, analyzing information at a high-level contra see fig. below

Sango: *na lége ni* "correctly, rightly," (lit. "by the way"; *lége* "road; path")

*hɪ-kɪkʷ- > *k̃ɪkʷ- "foot, leg"; Somali *lug* "leg, foot," Kikongo (Kitunda dialect) *-léng-* "walk," *-léeng-* "leap"; PB **-denge* "foot, leg" (Meeussen).

$m3^c.t$ = m-r-k-t = m-$k̃ɪkʷ$-t

More Africa association of ideas –

In the three pictures below, the first one is from Bugwere; seated on the left hand side of Itulula is Ikumbania sitting on the Throne with an Oxtail in his right hand, comparable with the middle picture at the top, we see a Diviner sitting on the Divine Mat, holding an Oxtail in her Right hand. Both are taken in modern Africa pschological time and space. At the bottom of the same picture we see Pharaonic pschological time and space – a seated Pharaonic Deity holding an Oxtail. In the third and final picture reveals association ideas; "knob Stick" association with a "sbA" = to instruct, to tend, to guide in Pharaonic pschological time and space. In modern Africa pschological time and space a knob stick association to Master, Elder, the Sadama etc.

Native Home base; Bugwere Community in Eastern Uganda, Bugwere Community is a member of Africa Great Lakes Region

The history of Bugwere is short and challenging. A majority Bagwere are said to have emigrated to their present area from Banyore and Toro, and travelled along Lake Kyoga, crossing River Mpologoma. For this reason, all the people that settled along the shores of Lake Kyoga like; Banyole, Baluli, Bakenye, Balamogi have a similar language fo Lugwere. Bugwere is also made up of Nilotic and Luo percentage. Bugwere initial area of settlement has shrunk considerably as the Iteso the Bagisu the Badama have pushed the Bagwere's frontiers inwards.

Sangoma

Asar Imhotep

Kemetic master-teacher

Sidama master-teacher, South Ethiopia

Author unknown

Challenge;

Now, the Subject of this Seminar is "Principles of Building Libraries in Rural Africa".

Quiz;

Do you think in the era of SDGs pschological Time and Space, Africa can tell Africa History properly if implementation of SDG4 quality education, does not emphasize Africa Spoken Languages union with Mother Language Kemet in Antiquity?

Chapter 7

The Way Forward; initiative in contributing to SDGs "future we want" –

Challenge;

Now, the Subject of this Seminar is "Principles of Building Libraries in Rural Africa".

Quiz;

Do you think in the era of SDGs pschological Time and Space, Africa can tell Africa History properly if implementation of SDG4 quality education, does not emphasize Africa Spoken Languages union with Mother Language Kemet in Antiquity?

Somewhere this Seminar proves that excellence is what we repeatedly do. The meaning of it is; we become good at things we do for ourselves. We become disoriented if someone is always doing things for us.

Here is the Scenario; implementation of SDG4 quality education must foster Start-up phase for Africa School Curriculum reform Year 2022

Year 2022, he or she who wants to enter to live, work and research in Africa must come with his or her certificate in introduction to Mother language; Ranykemet. In case of families entering Africa have minors, they will be taught in school following the school curriculum.

This social research began with introduction of the Subject of the book, the aim and now Chapter 7; has announced; Excellence is the Goal, which cannot be if Africa School Curriculum Reform is not in place. The rest of Chapter 7 will briefly summarise all the chapters of the book. Ahead of the introduction please find the Declaration, ahead of the Dedication and Acknowledgement. This research is dedicated to "Our Youths Who Carry the Promise for Tomorrow. Helping Africa States and Governments and initiative to contribution to SDGs. Next to the acknowledgment, is the Abbreviations page followed by a page of Transliteration from Ranykemet; Mother Language to English Spoken Language.

This book is made up of 7 Chapters. Chapter 1. is brief given definition of the Project/ social research initiative, a contribution to SDGs, where chapter 1 also begins with the question; "why Bugwere folklore Saaga" this is to motivate the reader towards the Aim the Objective, and the Strategy to the Goal. Chapter2. Brings on the research Context; Historical Africa; a Philosophical People with resource inherent in the culture. This ensured that the graduates were well prepared to be resilient in weathering the inevitable tests of life that come in the form of life's hardships. This is not the case of the typical graduate of the current African education system. Because the inclination is to look for help from outside Africa. sadly, this is the case whether that graduate is in or outside Africa. Chapter 2 does not round off until it explains how Historical Africa is the Source of Birth of Knowledge, how this happened, and how the Africa visitors to Africa in Antiquity went there in purposely, to drink at the Fountain of knowledge, and when they brought back this knowledge to their indigenous home Nations. That incentivized the Rebirth of Knowledge Custom. Many before having gone back to Africa to drink from the Fountain of Knowledge, Africa deserves this chance in the era of SDGs Pschological Time and Space.

Rebirth of Knowledge

- Rebirth of knowledge is custom. In the era of SDGs Pschological Time and Space, Africa Sankofa, go back to the Source to get The Skills Right is
  Custom

Custom/ common law must not be confused or interchanged with "tradition" as we pointed out in Chapter 2 – the Context.

Chapter 3. is the place where this research places the Lore gathering. Chapter three is also where the research assembles the Project starts-up phase of information seminar work/ sensitization. Chapter 3 is where the seminar marge Bugwere lore and linguistics from other pschological time and space. The seminars of Chapter 3. do a good job of shading light of how Chapter 4; the Methodology Chapter. And again chapter 3 sheds light on the rest of the Chapters of this book; how each chapter will challenge and illuminate each other.

Chapter 4; this being a social research by political philosophy amateurs. It is easily noticeable from the Identified research questions and their Assumptions that the Research aims for Goal of the Target groups who the reader should by now have a clue who these target people are, in any case here is a quick remainder – Target groups; the Youths, helping Africa States and Governments and initiatives contributing to the implementation of the SDGs. The Goal of the target groups is "future we want" therefore the identified questions and their assumptions fit with philosophizing in society. To consider that; implementation of SDG4 quality education by 2030 for Africa it means School Core-Curriculum Reform. Not only to foster the Subject of this research and that is "the Principles of Building Local Libraries in Rural Africa" but also to foster Africa Spoken languages reunion with Mother Language in Antiquity. Not only, Political life in Africa need not to remove the sitting leadership and replace with modern Africa youths or graduate. What Africa needs is a School curriculum of Africa Worldview. Chapter 4. Identified research questions and their assumptions argue corruption is not a culture. Corruptions or racism the two are two sides of the same coin embedded in development aid a strategy of Intellectual Acrobatic, also refer to Eric Hobsbawm and Terence the authors of "inversion of traditions PDF 1983" explain this very plainly and precisely. Cheikh Anta Diop and Theophile Obenga symposia in UNESCO-Cairo conference 1974 is reference also in regard – "future we want".

Chapter 5; findings and results, this is the research's excellence start-up phase with findings and results, in fact a continuity from literature gathering and identified research questions. Chapter 5 shows-off the attractiveness of studying and examining phenomenal words related to pschological time and space... the way the research sees it; the Challenge of putting in place the Principles of building local libraries in Africa is Fierce, but the incentive comes from Africa people themselves need to learn mother language if Africa is to tell Africa history properly. Consequently, will see herself Africa walk into quality jobs is the courage to bring forth the research finding; initiatives contributing to the implementation of the SDGs

Think of; every educated person can claim to know what is called a library, or what an Art Gallery stands for. What a Museum is etc. nonetheless, in our period of life, such buildings are meaningless to modern African until Africa Spoken languages union with Mother Language in Antiquity are studied and written down by Africa people themselves.

Meaning that a language or African nation(s) writing down Africa spoken languages independent of comparative method, is a risk because without a comparative method the language(s) in question remain marginalize. Development aid to Africa the last ca. 200 years, firstly by the missionaries, followed by colonialism and modern NGOs development aid. The strategy is not minus Marginalizing Africa Spoken Language. This is not good because this phenomenon holds Africa prisoners of marginalized jobs. But holding people in marginalized jobs is not "future we want".

Chapter 6; is the books hub for discussion and workshop, this Project does so with insight and tribute to the first spoken language on Mother Knee; Lugwere folklore. Participating in lore is warm and attractive due to the simplicity of the lives of the folk telling the lore.

Chapter 6. set up of Discussion/ workshop is to prompt Rural Africa get ready for School Curriculum year 2022 in our pschological time and space of SDG4 quality education in Africa. the World is past the pschological time and space when the World considered Africa as incapable of producing anything that may be considered Civilization – in the Chapter 6 with reference to Association of Ideas extracted from the book Comparative

Methods by Jean Claude Mboli 2010. Brings out evidence from Historical Africa archives Africa is the Birth of Knowledge where everyone returns to drink from Fountain of Knowledge.

Twasonga Mbele[7] – "future we want"

---

[7] Twasonga mbele is Swahili word or phrase meaning – the way forward.

References;

▢ How language came to man in Africa – linguistic Comparative Method; Jean Claude Mboli 2010

▢ A beginner's introduction to sSw mdw nTr; Royal Scribes in Kemet Hieroglyphs transliteration
and translation; Wudjau Iry Maat; 2015

▢ Africa Oral Literature; Isidore Okpewho 1992

▢ http://staff.washington.edu/ellingsn/Hobsbawm_Inventing_Traditiions.pdf
▢ https://sustainabledevelopment.un.org/index.php?menu=1298
▢ http://www.vukadarkie.com/cheikh-anta-diop-1974-unesco-symposium-in-cairo/

Biographies

- https://www.youtube.com/watch?v=Q5Gk36pUu1k

  28th Nov 2017 Uppsala University Lecture on Africa Poverty
- https://www.youtube.com/watch?v=vCm0JlGapP4

  Africa What to Demand 2018; conversation with sn. Mulocho Eric and snr.t wr.t Biibbi
- https://www.youtube.com/watch?v=x-dKbi-qOLg

  How Africa Culture History Matters
- https://www.youtube.com/watch?v=LcEDSmm56mc

  Jan 2018 Racism debate by Johan Galtung Q and A
  The video removed, by the debate management?

- https://www.youtube.com/watch?v=UiqUtVRd6DY
  The Great Nile Valley on Global Cardinal Orientation; by Wudjau Iry Maat 2017

- https://www.youtube.com/watch?v=VUZ_-bUrTNs
  NUPI; Oslo Norway; Foreign Affairs Debate 15th March 2018

- https://kunde.180.no/kp/default.asp?cmd=bilder&9hb9ek2c8wmdia408d8s